First hand accounts of the Syrian refuge experiences in Lesvos, Idomeni, and Eko camps in Greece from October 2015 through February 2017. Medical practitioners and humanitarian workers from the US, Jordan, and Syria as well as refuges themselves bring to life the refugee crisis in Greece.
—Linda Sartor, *Turning Fear into Power*

Richard Falk is the co-author or co-editor of forty books. In 2008, The United Nations Human Rights Council (UNHRC) appointed Falk to a six-year term as a United Nations Special Rapporteur on human rights in the occupied Palestinian territories. Here is a letter from Richard Falk:

Dear Bill and Madi:

I extend my great admiration for you and colleagues for making this effort on behalf of the refugees in Greece and deep gratitude that you and your crew took the trouble to share your experience with the rest of us. It is extremely important to have the benefit of this concrete witnessing, especially given the present political atmosphere.

With warm greetings,

Richard Falk

An invaluable collection of harrowing first-hand accounts by volunteer health workers. *Leaving Syria* reveals the tragic plight of those Syrian refugees lucky enough to make it across the sea to Greece. The authenticity and empathy of these informed witnesses is especially crucial at a time when the suffering of refugees from Islamic war-torn regions is too often disregarded by politicians and treated as a bothersome statistic by the media.
—Richard Falk, Emeritus Professor, Princeton

During the years that we spent under the war . . .
We knew that the guns can kill . . .
We knew that the planes can kill . . .
Chemical weapons can kill . . .
We escaped to find our life, but we found that the sea can
    kill . . .
Survived from the sea, to find that the borders can kill . . .
Share our suffering . . .
Make the world know . . .
    —Amer al-Haj

We all see the horrendous pictures in the newspaper and on TV. But the gap between a picture and reality is left to the imagination. *Leaving Syria* is a first-hand account that brings alive the plight of Syrian and other refugees caught in Greece: the pain, pathos, fear, and exhaustion. Simply stunning. No one reading this book can come away unmoved.

    —Jim McDermott, Congressman (retired)

Front Cover (top): A rubber raft crowded with Syrian refugees drifts in the Aegean between Turkey and Greece after its motor broke down off the Greek island of Kos. August 11, 2015.
Front Cover (bottom): Syrian refugees carry a child from a rubber raft after arriving at the Greek island of Lesvos after crossing the Aegean from Turkey.
Back Cover: Moria refugee camp, Lesvos, Greece. March 2, 2016.

Leaving Syria

This book is dedicated to those who have decided that the world is a far better place when we work to build bridges rather than fences.

LEAVING SYRIA

The Plight of Refugees
Stranded in Greece

**Bill Dienst, MD &
Madi Williamson**

Leaving Syria:
The Plight of Refugees Stranded in Greece
by Bill Dienst, MD & Madison Williamson
© 2017 Bill Dienst, MD & Madi Williamson
Cune Press, Seattle 2017
First Edition

Hardback	ISBN 9781614571810	$29.95
Paperback	ISBN 9781614571827	$19.95
Kindle	ISBN 9781614571841	$ 9.99

NGO Disclaimer: See page 147
Maps: Jim Williamson
Cover photos:
front cover by Yannis Behrakis / Reuters
back cover by Anjo Kan / Shutterstock

 Aswat: Voices from a Small Planet (a new series from Cune Press)

Looking Both Ways	Pauline Kaldas
Stage Warriors	Sarah Imes Borden
Stories My Father Told Me	Helen Zughraib

 Syria Crossroads (a series from Cune Press)

The Plain of Dead Cities	Bruce McLaren
Steel & Silk	Sami Moubayed
Syria - A Decade of Lost Chances	Carsten Wieland
The Road from Damascus	Scott C. Davis
A Pen of Damascus Steel	Ali Ferzat
Leaving Syria	Bill Dienst, MD & Madi Williamson
Visit the Old City of Aleppo	Khaldoun Fansa
East of the Grand Umayyad	Sami Moubayed
White Carnations	Musa Rahum Abbas

 Bridge Between the Cultures (a series from Cune Press)

Child Labor	Thinh Nguyen
The Other Side of the Wall	Richard Hardigan
Turning Fear Into Power	Linda Sartor
Apartheid is a Crime	Mats Svensson
A Year at the Edge of the Jungle	Frederic Hunter
The Girl Ran Away	Frederic Hunter

 Cune Press: www.cunepress.com | www.cunepress.info

Contents

Illustrations

A Note to the Reader

THIS BOOK IS A COLLECTION of first-hand accounts of the current crisis among refugees and the wider effect on Greece itself. Most of the refugees are Syrian, but there are also substantial populations of Kurds and Yazidis from Syria and Iraq. There are also other Iraqis, as well as Afghans and Pakistanis. There are refugees of other nationalities too.

Our authors are health care and other humanitarian volunteers who have been there. They have written, for the most part, in the present tense . . . to give the reader a feel for the reality that our authors saw and touched when they lived and worked among the refugees. The delay between actual events and writing about them varies with each chapter. Some were written within a week of the time that the events occurred, while others were written as long as a year afterward. Please note that the terms "Lesvos" and "Lesbos" refer to the same Greek island.

I
On the Island of Lesvos

Young woman on the beach near Mytilini, Lesvos, 2016.

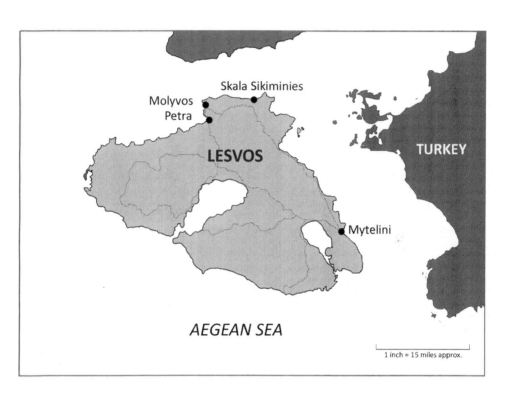

1
Mass Casualties

October 5, 2015
Lesvos, Greece
Jamal Sawalha
(Jamal Sawalha is from Jordan, working as the logistics manager for Salaam Cultural Museum in Greece.)

IT IS 12:00 NOON, AND I HAVE JUST LANDED WITH MY FATHER at the airport, a little south of Mytilene, which is the capital of the Greek Island of Lesvos. We are here to volunteer with Salaam Cultural Museum. SCM is a small Non-Governmental Organization run by our extended family members and others who are based in Jordan and the USA. During the past several years, we have been providing medical and humanitarian relief to Syrian refugees in Jordan and Lebanon. Now there are growing numbers of refugees here in Greece with growing needs too, and we are here to assess how we can help. I plan to be here in Lesvos for a couple of weeks and then head back to Jordan.

We are waiting for the rental company to bring us a nine-seater van that we will be using to run our operations while we are here. While my father deals with the car rental company, I wait outside the airport. I see many people walking from the beach, past the airport, and toward the city center of Mytilene. They look like refugees; they are wet and appear confused: they don't seem to know what to do or where they are going. Finally at 2:00 pm, we get our van. Now we are heading north to meet our colleague: another volunteer who has already been here for some time, so he can show us around.

We drive to the north shore of the Island of Lesvos. This is where most of the refugees are crossing the Aegean Sea from Turkey, because these northern straights are the narrowest crossing point: only ten km. As we drive north, we see hundreds and hundreds more refugees walking south towards Mytilene. From the north shore, this is a walking distance of about seventy km. The refugees have to come to Mytilene to register. Then they stay in a large transition camp for several days. Once they obtain the proper paper work, they board ferries to the Greek mainland, and then they make their way further north through the Balkans to their ultimate destinations in northern and Western Europe.

October 12, 2015

Days are running rapidly together. After only a week here, I have quickly concluded that two weeks will not be enough time. Refugees continue arriving on Lesvos from Turkey in huge numbers. Some days, Lesvos receives up to 10,000 people per day. There aren't enough volunteers to cover their needs. I just extended my Visa to the end of December so I can continue working here.

October 28, 2015

The alarm clock sounds: it's 7:00 am, and time to wake up! But I am tired. Last night was long. Oxy is a makeshift camp; it is a holding area that has been set up in a parking lot next to an abandoned nightclub. We have been helping there. The night clinic stayed open until 1:30 am due to late boat arrivals, so I didn't get much sleep. It takes me ten minutes to fully wake up. I am finally feeling ok. Now I am with the team having breakfast as usual and getting ready to head back to our 7:30-10:00 am shift at Oxy Camp.

But this does not happen. Our breakfast gets cut short because we have spotted a boat about to land near the Panselinos Hotel where we are staying. We quickly divert our van to the shore to make sure that we are there before the boat arrives. We want to make sure that we can lead the approaching boat to a safer spot to land. The beach is not flat and there are dangerous rocky outcroppings. This boat lands safely. People are terrified, the sea is rough, all of them are cold, and soaking wet. We arrange transportation to the Oxy camp with other volunteers and then head directly to the camp ourselves.

All of the refugees who have arrived on the shore are now at the camp and getting new dry clothes as well as sandwiches and fruit. We start screening the refugees for medical needs. Luckily this time, the cases that we see are limited to just coughs and colds. Since I have arrived here on October 5th, the International Rescue Committee (IRC) has now arranged bus services to Mytilene, which saves refugees the exhausting seventy km walk. The refugees already have their bus tickets and are waiting for their turn to head to the official camps to get registered and take their papers.

Now it's 10:00 am, and we are on our way back to the hotel to finish our breakfast, so we can continue our day with full power. We will then continue to patrol the beaches, on the lookout for new boats approaching from Turkey.

The next two hours seem calm compared to what we have become used to. Then at noon, I get a call from Melinda, in Molyvos-the largest town near us on the north shore of Lesvos. Melinda is the founder of the humanitarian NGO called Starfish. She is requesting immediate full medical assistance at the port. She sounds extremely worried. I drive as fast as I can toward the port across dirt roads. On my way, I see a doctor I know from the Dutch NGO, Boat Refugee Foundation, and pick him up. Neither of us knows the full extent of the current situation.

As I negotiate the delicate narrow medieval streets of central Molyvos toward the harbor with my huge van, we see that the coast guard ship is rushing to the harbor. It appears that they are bringing us some medical cases. We assume that it will be as usual: wet people from a distressed boat. But it's much worse than that. We arrive just as the Greek Coast Guard ship docks. Sailors are yelling, "Doctor, Doctor!" It turns out that they are bringing in refugees from a boat that flipped over because of the waves. Among many needing medical attention, they bring one father and two kids that appear to have drowned. The coast guard ship drops off all the refugees and heads back out to sea again.

The two children are not breathing. Their father is barely moving and suffering from hypothermia. The medical team is taking care of the kids and performing CPR while I am alongside other volunteers trying to warm the man. He is shivering and screaming. For me this is extremely stressful: my first time seeing such a thing. Unfortunately, the younger child is dead; he was probably already more than fifteen minutes dead before we received him. Nothing can be done. His older sister is responding to the CPR. It is emotionally gratifying to see her coming back to life.

The father is now regaining consciousness. He is becoming aware of what is happening. He is going crazy with grief, asking about his kids and not yet knowing what happened to his boy. We are doing what we can to try to console him, but it's not working. It's a really heart-wrenching moment: the father is yelling and shouting at his son to wake up. He is trying to perform Cardiopulmonary Resuscitation (CPR) but it's not working either. We know that and anyone can know that just by looking at the color of the body. But nothing can stop any father in such a situation.

Finally, after a while, the ambulance is here and the father is still trying to bring his son back to life. The ambulance drives all three of them to the hospital, which is over 1 hour away in Mytilene. We are all sitting there, devastated.

We finally decide to head back to the hotel and call it a day. We are not in the mood to do anything else, especially after witnessing all this. We are trying to pull ourselves together and debrief. We remind ourselves that we did our best, and we could not do anything further to change the outcome.

But as it turns out, this is not anywhere near the end of our day. Now, it's 5:30 pm. After several hours of intense melancholy, we finally all agree that we need to head out again to do some beach patrolling. Perhaps it might change our mood a little bit.

We are driving east from Eftalou Beach, which is the beginning of the dirt road. It climbs to the top of a high hillside near the eastern edge of Zone 1 where SCM is responsible. We see a Greek Coast Guard ship rushing at high speed to the west in the direction of Molyvos port with a lot of orange vests onboard. It is unusual to see the coast guard moving that fast when they are transporting refugees. We scan the seas with our binoculars to find out if there are any boats in distress. One of the volunteers spots some lifejackets in the sea. I look through the binoculars and see what looks like three refugees in the sea. Later on, we will find out that there were many more than three.

We decide that the best thing to do is to head to the harbor, since we are also the medical team covering the harbor area in Molyvos. It's now 5:50 pm; we have made it half way back to Molyvos harbor. My phone rings; it's Melinda. It is not good. Her plea is, "Jamal! Bring all available doctors and come to the harbor now!"

Based on the position of the coast guard ship, it appears we have a five-minute window. We quickly stop by the Panselinos Hotel (where we are staying) on our way to the harbor. We grab the extra oxygen tanks that we have. In less than a minute, we are off on the road again. As we approach the restaurant area in the middle of Molyvos, we see the same doctor from the Boat Refugee Foundation again walking alongside the road. "Get in the Van now!" I scream. He asks, "What's going on?"

"They need all available doctors at the harbor now, so please jump in." Again, I am driving my huge van through the delicate narrow medieval streets of Molyvos toward the harbor, but this time, I'm driving like a maniac. We somehow manage to arrive before the coast guard, which gives us a few moments to prepare our equipment for the second potential mass casualty incident today.

We are at the harbor now and Melinda is there. It's much bigger than the first incident. "We don't know how many people, but there are a lot of drownings," she reports. "A big boat just capsized but we don't have all the information yet. The first coast guard ships and other rescue boats are on their way now."

Everything is now setup: from oxygen tanks to Automated Electronic Defibrillators. The doctors are splitting into teams with nurses and paramedics. All of this is happening extremely fast.

A lot of people are starting to gather in the marina to see what is going

Refugees arriving from Turkey. North coast of Lesvos near Molyvos, Lesvox, 2015.

on. And now here is the first coast guard ship entering the harbor. But there are a lot of smaller boats inside the harbor that are in the way. This ancient harbor, crowded with fishing vessels and pleasure craft, is not equipped to handle a massive rescue operation such as this. So the coast guard ship seizes the opportunity to dock alongside a fishing boat that was docked at the pier next to the restaurants.

Several volunteers, a couple of doctors and I jump on the fishing boat. We help the coast guard sailors unload and transport the refugees off the ship, across the middle of the fishing boat, and onto the pier: the sick and injured, the walking wounded, and the drowned.

It's extremely difficult. The people we unload from the boat, if not drowned, are very hypothermic. It's one horrible tragedy after another. A lot of people are milling about, just gawking. The media are on the way to get the scoop; no one knows how they arrive so fast. All this chaos complicates the efforts of the rescue workers.

The medical team attempts CPR on several drowning victims. We are equipped to handle a few cases; but the sheer volume leaves us overwhelmed. We wait for ambulances for those we successfully resuscitate, but who are still critically injured. But the ambulances are taking a very long time.

A lot of the refugees are asking for relatives . . . their kids or their wives. Several wives are screaming and crying for their husbands. I am one of the few rescuers that can speak Arabic. This adds more stress for me than what it is already apparent: everyone attempts to speak and understand everyone else through me all at once.

One lady is looking for her husband. His name is Omar. They just got married recently, and now she can't find him. She is crying and screaming. A lot of the international rescuers can't understand exactly what is going on because of the language barrier. She was picked up by one rescue boat, but not with her man. Now she is freaking out and starts running around looking for him. But no one knows where he is or even what he looks like. I am trying to calm her down. I promise her that we will find him. But sadly, it's really hard to tell if he is dead, if he is among the rescued at the harbor or what.

There are a lot of refugees. We still don't even have a clear understanding of what exactly has happened. Many refugees who can walk are brought to the Captain's Table (a small restaurant that Melinda owns; also a place where all the volunteers gather to eat and socialize, when things are calm). Other refugees are taken to the gallery near the harbor and some have been put in the small church nearby.

While we are looking for Omar the husband, an Iraqi family stops me and asks if they can use my phone to call their family back in Iraq to inform them that they arrived and survived this incident. I give them my phone. They try calling using the online app called Viper.

I use this as our opportunity to find out what actually happened to them out at sea. It turns out that they were smuggled on a wooden boat and were forced along with many others to get on that boat which was overloaded with about 300 refugees. They told me that the boat actually broke in the middle of the sea, due to the combined forces of the heavy weight and the heavy waves.

The overloaded second floor of the boat collapsed on top of the first floor, and then the whole boat broke into pieces, leaving all the refugees trying to float in the cold ocean waters with their fake life jackets that they had on, with little buoyancy.

Everyone was shivering and screaming; everyone was desperately trying to hold onto something or to someone. They have lost all their belongings: from passports and mobile phones to money; even their backpacks. All that they have left are the wet clothes that they are wearing. While I am still talking to them, the next coast guard ship arrives; but this time with their loudspeakers calling out for immediate help.

The first ship is still docked. There is no place to dock the second ship on the main pier. So it just weighs anchor and ties up to some floating wooden piers that are designed for small boats. They are not equipped to handle such a ship. But there is no other option. The ship is now immediately opposite the restaurant area, as this is the only area where there is space.

This new situation does not look good either. There are a lot of kids and babies onboard just lying there. Luckily, more doctors have now arrived. Over seven kids suffering from respiratory distress are tended to. One of the coast guard sailors is asking for a blanket and a doctor to board the ship. A moment later, the doctor comes out carrying a female teenager with clothing removed wrapped in the dry blanket, severely hypothermic.

Now another situation is brought my attention: An Iraqi guy is stepping down from the ship holding his kid and crying out loud, "He is dead! He is dead!" Quickly, the doctor grabs the kid from him and start performing CPR. I bring a chair for the father and another volunteer brings blankets. He is crying and asking about his kid, his wife and his other daughter. Nobody knows anything about their whereabouts, whether they have made it or not.

I am providing translation and support for this Iraqi man. It has now already been over ten minutes of CPR. One of doctors on my team informs me that there is still a chance that he will survive. But it's low. The father believes that he has already lost his child and he is becoming even crazier with grief. I am trying to calm him down. I see a response in the child. I gesture to the doctor and ask if the kid is responding and he replies, "Yes."

In the middle of this stressful moment, matters are made even worse. A cameraman with his huge video camera stumbles into one of the doctors who is trying to perform CPR. He is trying to take a video without thinking about what is he doing. Another volunteer sees this and pulls him away, making the cameraman angry. Luckily, a police officer sees what's happening and kicks all the media people out of the way from the rescue area where the doctors are working. After twenty minutes, the child is now responsive and the team is trying to keep him stable until the ambulance comes. There is a big shortage of ambulances. We are told that on the whole island of Lesvos, there are only three ambulances operating.

In the meantime, other volunteers just found this Iraqi man's wife and his daughter. Luckily, they were in the gallery. Soon they are with us. We are reassuring all of them that his child is improving and that the ambulance is on its way. This helps the man to slowly calm down.

But wait! It's not over yet. We just got a call from Frontex (the marine border patrol for the European Union). They will be sending the rest of the refugees, both the rescued and the drowned, on ships to Petra Port. This port is an industrial port. It has one large long linear pier, and it is in a guarded area. Though it is a ten-minute drive from here southwest of Molyvos town and a bit further away from the location of the accident, it's much better equipped toward staging mass casualties such as this; and it is much easier for large ships to dock. The harbor of Molyvos can't take any more large ships at this time. It is packed with people and the access to the port is really congested due to the heavy traffic. So now we divide up our teams. Some continue in Molyvos, while the rest of the medics pile into vans with medical equipment and rapidly drive to Petra Port.

Moments after we arrive, the Frontex people direct us towards two kids onboard their ship, which is now docked. We quickly rush onboard the big Frontex ship to assist. But it's really tragic to see them lying on the ship's deck. As the medics attempt resuscitation, I stand for a few seconds in shock just staring at the kids. I know instinctively that they are already dead, and we won't be able to do anything about it. Soon, the doctors confirm this and tell the Frontex sailors that they are already dead, that they have been dead for a while now. I still can't forget the look of the two children; their skin color and faded look in their eyes.

This has been by far the worst shock of my life. It's the first time I have ever seen, not just one dead child, but three. Yes, three innocent children whose only fault was to be born in war zones . . . kids who died because their parents were trying to escape to a safer country, hoping to ensure a better life for them.

Several days later, I remain in a funk of emotional despair. October 28, 2015 will remain a day that I will never forget. This is a day that will change my whole perspective on life; a day that will make me change the focus of my career. I will keep on doing humanitarian aid. The 28th of October: a black day for Lesvos and a black day in the memory of everyone who experienced it.

2
Rescues

Southern Greece
Amer al-Haj
(Amer al-Haj is one of thousands of Syrian refugees stranded in Greece.)

Please Don't Cry

One second at the camp's clinic

A familiar medication handed to the man whose request I translate

Two minutes on the shores of Izmir

Some day in February, on a cold night, one o'clock after midnight

A woman in her twenties . . . a small child in her arms . . .one-year-old, maybe?

Wakes up from his sleep, begins to weep

The cry breaks the dark . . . shakes the invisible snake, moving towards the rubber boat on the beach

Quiet! We must be quiet. Silence in our steps. Loud are the baby's screams. It grows.

The head of the line stops. We obey.

We all stand, silent, motionless.

The smuggler's pocket produces a small box. He walks up to the woman and the little boy. "Give him ten drops to sleep."

This stuns everyone. Yet, no one speaks a word, no one opposes.

Even if they wanted to, they wouldn't. We are in pitch darkness. They have their feelings, although you won't see crying, laugher or anger.

I am near the woman. She opens the canister. "Will he wake up again if I give him ten?" One second it would take me to reassure her. Answer yes. But the word chokes up in my throat

Because I do not really understand what is going on.

The smuggler's voice speaks before I can.

"Of course he will. We give some children more than that. Let's hurry."

The woman sits on the ground . . . tries to force the child who resists the medicine. He does not want to be part of this crime. Her hands shake. Her breath is troubled.

I am called to help them finish. I approach them and grab the boy with the mother. Together we pour the blobs into his mouth. The cries have not increased, but the screaming has.

I still see the woman's face today. Her eyes filled with tears when forced to drug her son. I still remember her fear.

Fear for her child. Fear of the sea.

And I wonder. Why does the enemy enter our land loud with planes, guns and explosions? But we, the land's owners, we have to leave in silent caution.

Even our children must not weep . . .

A young girl in Eko camp, located a few kilometers down the highway from the Greece/Macedonia border.

© Abdulazez Dukhan

December 20, 2015
Molyvos, Lesvos
Raafia Gheewala, Pharm D
(Dr Gheewala is an East Indian-American pharmacist from Massachusetts, volunteering with SCM.)

My first few days here are a mix of emotions. I am witnessing firsthand the struggles that the refugees are enduring every step of the way.

The town of Molyvos in the Northwest corner of Lesvos is a beautiful romantic honeymoon destination, with quaint charm on every street. It has now become infiltrated with Non-Governmental Organizations from all over the world volunteering to help. Lesvos is the first point of entry into Europe for thousands of refugees coming ashore.

Before I arrived here, I was trying to prepare myself for what I would witness, but words cannot do justice to the emotions that I feel. Every man and woman, young and old, has a story and has their dreams. Some want to head to Switzerland, some Sweden, and some don't care where they go as long as it's better for their family. Even so, most are living day to day.

The rescue infrastructure here has been rapidly evolving during the previous few months. Currently, the northern shore of Lesvos, where most of the refugees are crossing the ten km channel from Turkey, is split into four sections. Different NGOs have taken on different responsibilities in their assigned region. As the raft boats filled with people come to shore, the lifeguards help pull them to safety. Then an NGO called Starfish works to register all of them. They deal with exhausted frightened people and language barriers. Other NGO's like "Drop in the Ocean" and "Team Humanity" are responsible for providing clothing, and another NGO called "Dirty Girls" launders the refugees' wet clothes and returns them. Salaam Cultural Museum (SCM) is the primary medical group in Zone 1; but we currently only have one doctor who's doing an amazing job attending to everyone in need. We are quickly learning that everything is a group effort.

The refugees arriving on shore are mainly from Syria although some come from Afghanistan. As we help pull the boats to shore, almost everyone is crying. We form a chain of volunteers to help the children off first and change them into warm, dry clothing. Then the adults come off. We rush to help them change, provide food and water, and handle any medical issues. They are hypothermic, weak, suffering from emotional shock, and some have injuries. What breaks my heart today is seeing grown men sobbing. They are happy that they made it with their family to Greece alive and safe, but they are also filled with anxiety about the rest of their unknown journey.

Every single person that I help is grateful. They are hugging me and kissing me and sending me prayers and love. The language barrier is an obstacle, but once I smile and say Salaam, a level of trust is built and we embrace each other. The children are beautiful with smiles that melt your heart. Their giggles ring in my ear as they play with the local cats, and show excitement from the toys or lollipops we give out. Mothers, fathers, and grandparents hug and kiss you like you are their own when you help them or their family. The teenagers want to take selfies and keep in touch via Facebook. There is an indescribable bond.

But not everything goes smoothly. There is an eight-month-pregnant woman who comes off the boat having contractions. She, her husband, and her in-laws thought it was better for her to risk all of their lives on the boat than to stay in Syria or Turkey. Just think about that.

Would you put your pregnant wife, daughter, or sister on a dinky raft boat across treacherous waters all through the night in hopes for a better life? Would you spend thousands of dollars for your family to take this boat ride across these dangerous currents in the Aegean straits, knowing that they could die at sea, in hopes for a better life? Would you leave your home, your friends, your pets, everything you've ever known, to come to a whole new country, not knowing your next move? Is it worth sleeping outside in the cold, eating one meal a day, and spending your life savings in hopes for a better life? This is happening and I am witnessing it every day with my own eyes. All I can do is to try to help make this moment in their lives a tiny bit less burdensome, make them feel human and welcome, and pray for their safety.

I think about myself, my family, and my friends. We have been so lucky and we are so blessed. But these people are just like us. Life has not been fair to them. They have worked hard to provide for their families, only to flee in the most tumultuous of circumstances.

Mothers and fathers worry about their children. Babies cling to their parents. Children sing songs and say that they can't wait to go back to school. They ask for so little, yet are so appreciative when we provide basic human needs.

In this short time, I already see a need for Arabic and Farsi speakers and translators. They will feel more welcome speaking their own language and will be provided quicker medical and humanitarian care if we can better address their language needs.

December 23, 2015

The past two days are a whirlwind; it feels like weeks have passed. Every time I think I have heard the most heartbreaking story ever, another family arrives with their own story, equally horrific. It's hard to stay strong for these refugees as they come off the boats from Turkey. But it's also amazing how your mind and body can turn into overdrive and not let your emotions take over. It's hard to differentiate who has it worse, because we only know parts of their stories and have no idea what else they have had to endure.

Many of these people have been beaten up, robbed, and have had guns and knives put to them or their families. They have been cheated and lied to in every way. Some of them have been cast off from shore in boats with not enough fuel to last the distance across and given fake life vests with inadequate buoyancy that are unsafe. They are so desperate to flee the turmoil in their own countries, that they are buying raft boats from gyro shops in Turkey.

They have been told that their journey should take twenty minutes, and begin to worry when it turns into hours. When they finally make landfall, they are freezing cold, soaking wet, and terrified. Some are separated from their families, or members of their families have died at sea. Everyone suffers from various degrees of emotional shock.

We have seen thousands of refugees from Syria, Iraq, and Afghanistan; also migrants from Pakistan, Iran, Somalia, and the Congo. The one thing they all have in common is their sincere gratitude. Everyone is constantly thanking us and sending us prayers. We hear them say that the volunteers they have encountered in Greece have been the kindest people they have ever encountered. They offer to give us jewelry off their body as tokens of appreciation and love. One grandmother even said to me and my team in Arabic, that if she could give us her eyes or hands or heart she would because that is all she has now, all while sending us constant prayers. The NGOs here are remarkable. I am truly blessed to have this opportunity to be a part of them.

December 28, 2015

My last few days in Lesvos are even more overwhelming than the first few. I am learning that for most of the refugees, it won't get much easier. It makes me really think about how horrible their lives must have been in their homeland to pick up and leave everything they ever knew. Some leave their families behind, starting over. They endure physical pain and anxiety every step of the way. There are several children sent with their aunts and uncles or other extended relatives. Some have been orphaned, or they are leaving parents behind in hopes of a better life. I see some families caring for their relatives' children like they are their own. But I also see others, those who have abandoned and robbed them. I see children who have witnessed their parents being taken or killed in front of their eyes. I hear stories about boats, whose passengers survived what were deliberate attempts to drown them.

I see wounds and bruising that make refugees want to escape so badly that they don't even care whether they stay in Greece forever. Every story pains my heart. I feel blessed to meet some of these refugees and hear their stories. I've met doctors, lawyers, and teachers: regular people just like me and you. I am learning a lot from them, about how little one really needs to survive and about what really is important in life.

They are teaching me the power of prayer. Some of them, especially the elderly, come off boats soaking wet and freezing. But many of them are also praying and thanking God for protecting them and their family; for keeping them alive. They are teaching me that faith, family, freedom, food, and shelter are the basics; all one really needs. I am seeing that children are very resilient.

I will never forget these children: the smiles on their faces, and their laughter as I play with them. I will never forget their sad expressions when I have to ration food and turn people away when we run out of supplies. I will never forget the feeling of hope they have as they arrive from Turkey. The faces of helpless exhausted families who have been robbed or beaten will forever stay with me. I pray that they all will be taken care of and that they make it to their final destination with minimal turmoil, and safely. I have seen some of their prayers answered and the joy on their faces when their registration is complete and they are allowed to leave to their next destination on the mainland of Greece. I hope they find peace and happiness in their new life.

Although my time here is now over, I am already trying to plan my return. There is so much to be done and so much more help is needed. I'd like to thank all of the volunteers across the world that really are working for humanity: people putting their lives on hold for weeks and months; people quitting their jobs and selling their homes to help this cause. It has truly been a beautiful experience with wonderful selfless people. I will never forget the friends I have here and the bonds that are being created while caring for the most vulnerable. My team is remarkable and they are doing great things during the most critical of times. I'd like to thank my big sister Rayesa, the best travel buddy I could have asked for, and without whom my experience wouldn't have been the same. Thanks for taking care of me, for being the mom of the team, and being my rock of sanity through it all.

Peace out Lesvos. Until next time.

3

Impasse

February 29, 2016
Panselinos Hotel, Lesvos
Bill Dienst, MD
(Dr Dienst is a rural family and emergency room physician from Washington volunteering as Medical Coordinator for SCM.)

I LANDED HERE ON THE NORTHERN SHORE of the Greek Island of Lesvos on 26 February. Lesvos is the third largest of the Greek Islands, and is the closest to the Turkish coast, separated on its northern coast by only six miles (ten km). For this reason, it has been the main crossing point for refugees.

It has been very quiet since I came here three days ago in terms of refugee boat arrivals on the northern coast. Currently, the Turkish Government, the Greek Government, the European Union and NATO are engaged in an elaborate political dance of Cat-and-Mouse with the human smugglers and refugees from Syria, Iraq, Afghanistan, Pakistan and other locations.

The refugees are intermittently stranded on the Turkish side. Their goal is to land in Greece, thereby entering the European Union, then making their way to the Greek mainland. From there, they try to travel overland through the former Yugoslavian republics of Macedonia, Serbia, Slovenia, and then onward to Austria, Germany, and other locations in northern Europe.

There are bottlenecks and various hardships along the way; e.g. the Former Yugoslavian Republic of Macedonia just started building a fence. There is a lot of uncertainty: hurry up, then wait, then hurry up again. For us rescuers, there is a need for flexibility and improvisation. During the past few months, there have been periods of working too hard, and then periods of hardly working. We are currently experiencing the latter, which gives me opportunity to write about this overall situation.

The goals of the "Powers That Be" are convoluted and confused: on the one hand they are trying their best to come to grips compassionately with the humanitarian catastrophe that endless wars have created in the troubled countries from whence the current refugees are fleeing. On the other hand, they must deal with the chaos and personal consequences of not knowing what to expect about massive immigration from the Near East and Africa: its immediate and long term effects on the previous ways of life for native citizens in the host countries, whose lives and economic well-being are also being affected.

Here on Lesvos, the economy has been based largely on agriculture, fishing, and tourism. The tourist season usually starts in the late spring, and lasts through September. The effects of the current refugee crisis have been tumultuous on the local economy. There have been both winners and losers, but the current overall perception among the local Greeks is that the overall effect on the economy will be a loss. Bookings for this summer's upcoming tourist season are down 80%. Tourists do not seem to want their restful summer escape from their hectic lives in the north of Europe to be interrupted by dead refugees washing ashore on the beach.

On the plus side, hotels and restaurants, usually moribund during the winter months, are currently fairly active, as they are being utilized by humanitarians and health care workers currently here to help the refugees. But these humanitarians do not spend their money as freely as the tourists. Some of the younger ones have been known to misbehave at times as well.

The refugees began arriving in large numbers this past October. Since then, various Non-Government-Organizations have arrived and infrastructures have evolved to provide services to refugees arriving from Turkey. They are based on the northern and eastern coasts of Lesvos located directly across from the Turkish coast. These NGOs have included the UN High Commission for Refugees (UNHCR), the International Rescue Committee (IRC), Medecins San Frontieres (MSF) or Doctors without Borders, and many others.

Here in the northern shore of Lesvos, we are divided into four zones of responsibility. I will be working in Zone 1 with a Seattle based NGO called Salaam Cultural Museum (SCM). We are comprised of both health care workers and humanitarians. Our members arrive for a week or longer assignments. I have decided to stay for two and a half months.

Our health care workers are aligned with a Norwegian group of Emergency Medical Technicians (EMT's and Paramedics) known as Medics Bergen. Our mission is largely pre-hospital care, triage, and acute/urgent care. We receive refugees at local beaches and docks. At the docks, they have usually been rescued at sea by the Greek Coast Guard or *Frontex*, the Border Control service of the European Union. Direct landings on the beaches and rock cliffs of the northern coast are much more dangerous.

There is an Italian NGO called Group Mission. They are currently in negotiations with the Greek Government, so that they can deploy a mobile Inten-

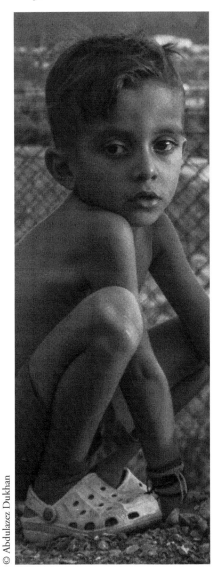

A young child greets visitors at the gate to a military camp located in Sindos just outside of Thessaloniki, Greece.

sive Care Unit. This would be helpful, as there are currently no hospital services on the north end of the Island. When boats capsize, there can be many emergencies all at once, and limited capacity in terms of health services.

There is only one medical clinic staffed part time by one Greek general practitioner a few days a week about ten kilometers away in the town called *Petra*. There are several doctors, nurses, EMT's, and others from around the world volunteering here on the north end of the Island, but serious limitations in terms of health care facilities. The nearest hospital is a one and a half hour drive away in Mytilene. Medecins sans Frontieres currently has two ambulances in our area when we have unstable patients who need transport to the hospital. Refugees arriving on the north coast are transferred promptly to the reception centers of Mora and Tara Kepe located near the capital Mytilene. This is where the hospital and most of the medical services are located.

In the next chapter, I will explain how the local system of receiving refugees on shore works.

4
Boat Refugees

March 5, 2016
The northern shore of Lesvos
Bill Dienst, MD

THE STRAITS BETWEEN TURKEY and the north shore of Lesvos have been a major route for human migration for hundreds of years. The present migration is nothing new; its uniqueness is only due to its magnitude, because of the current humanitarian crises caused by poverty and war. In late October 2015, over 7000 refugees crossed in boats during one 24-hour period, mostly across the northern route. On March 1, about 1450 people crossed, mainly in the south end of the island, due in large part to naval pressures in the north, which are trying to prevent these crossings.

As a direct result of tremendous humanitarian needs, many Non-Governmental Organizations have come to Lesvos, and systems for providing first response/medical relief have evolved.

There are two watchtowers along the north coast, where volunteers use infrared binoculars at night to spot incoming boats full of refugees. They are reinforced by a radio tower run by Medecins sans Frontieres (Doctors without Borders) which provides communications between refugee boats, lifeguard units on rescue boats, and the coast guard in the event of a maritime emergency. When boats are spotted, a system of text messaging is activated, giving international teams on shore the estimated time and location of arrival. These on-call teams of humanitarians and medical relief personnel are activated and then they respond to these locations. Frequently, refugee boats are intercepted by the Greek Coast Guard or other agencies such as Frontex, the customs and border protection ships with international crews. They represent the European Union. These ships then bring the refugees indirectly into the harbors, since direct landings on the northern beaches are treacherous.

As refugees disembark, they are greeted by a medical triage team and translators. Various degrees of hypothermia are by far the most common medical concern, so warming blankets, hand warmers, and removal of wet clothing are paramount. People are given water and transferred to an overnight camp by bus, with special concern for keeping families together and reuniting those who have become separated. Acute medical conditions are treated on site and ambulance evacuation is available if necessary. This is what happens during a routine arrival.

In cases of a Mass Casualty Incident (boat capsizing, drownings and near-drownings being the most common) a triage system based on international norms has been developed. In this case, a primary triage officer meets arrivals being taken off the boat or ship, and sorts them into categories. Red indicates in need of Emergency Care for immediate life or limb threatening conditions. Yellow means in need of Urgent Care, but can wait a bit. Green means those with no medical issues or those with minor medical issues that can wait longer. And Blue/Black indicates those who are dead, or who suffer such devastating injuries that further resuscitative care is deemed futile. Emergent life and limb threatening conditions are treated as they are identified, and suspected fractures are splinted.

A system of secondary triage is also implemented as patients can deteriorate or improve and change from one category to another. Emergency care is given on site, and patients needing inpatient care are transferred to the hospital an hour and a half away by either ambulance or private vehicle, depending of the seriousness and urgency of their condition and the ambulance resources available at a particular time.

Our team, Salaam Cultural Museum is allied with a Norwegian Team called Medics Bergen. We have a medical van that is equipped with warming supplies, wound care and splinting devices. We also have acute care medications such as treatments for asthma, antibiotics, gastrointestinal complaints, allergies, etc. We also have basic life support equipment such as airway supplies, IV fluids and Automated External Defibrillators (AEDs).

5
Across the Straits

March 7, 2016
Lesvos
Bill Dienst, MD

DAVID ENG, THE STARFISH HARBOR MASTER in charge of refugee operations on Molyvos Harbor on the north coast of Lesvos, calls me at 5:45 am. "There is a boat with about one-hundred refugees at sea being rescued by the Greek Coast Guard. We need you to assemble your team and meet us in Molyvos Harbor in twenty minutes."

In the darkness of early morning, I assemble my team: Salaam Cultural Museum medics, currently two doctors and one nurse. We also activate humanitarian volunteers, several with critical skills of speaking Arabic and Urdu. We arrive just in time to meet the Greek Coast Guard ship in the harbor at early dawn. We hear later that another refugee boat had been turned back toward Turkey by the Turkish Coast Guard. Turkey is now under tremendous pressure by the European Union to prevent refugee crossings to Greece.

As the ship arrives, we identify seventy-eight refugees, mostly Afghans who speak Pashtu and Dari; but can also understand some Urdu. There are also some Iraqis who speak Arabic. Overall, the refugees are in pretty good condition as they disembark: Welcome to Europe!

A little cold but not too wet; some are suffering from panic episodes, some have been separated from other family members who were put on the other rescue ship during the confusion when the rescue ships first arrived. The other rescue ship was sent to another harbor (Skala Sikaminias), located an hour away on a bumpy mountainous dirt road.

Through our Urdu and Arabic translators, we have to insist multiple times to those missing their loved ones that they get into the vans that will take them to the receiving camp at *Apanemo*, which is run by the International Rescue Committee (IRC). One Afghan woman insists she is not moving until we find her husband. We reassure her that she will find him at the IRC camp; we are probably right but not certain, but that is the best that can be hoped for. Apanemo is where the other arrivals from the other rescue boat that went to Skala Sikaminias will also go.

Debra, our nurse-midwife evaluates two pregnant women initially thought to be in early labor. They are OK; they board the evacuation vans with the others without incident. One woman who is suffering from a severe panic attack slowly improves with verbal reassurance that everything will be OK; for the moment. The next chapter in the long ordeal for these refugees is just beginning.

Apanemo is the temporary receiving camp where refugees arriving from shore are taken by the IRC vans. There, they receive food, clothing and water. A makeshift clinic is there to do secondary medical evaluations. Later in the day, refugees will be transported down to Moria or Tara Kepe, the camps near Mytilene, the capital of Lesvos. When refugees arrive in Moria, they are sorted into Arabic speakers, mainly Syrians and Iraqis, and the others, mainly Afghans, but also Kurds, Yazidis, Pakistanis, and several other ethnicities. Some of the Syrian and Iraqi families have the option of going to Tara Kepe, which is less crowed and better equipped.

6
Moria Camp

March 9, 2016
Moria Camp, near Mytilene, Lesvos
Kirsten Senturia, PhD
(Dr Senturia is a medical anthropologist from Washington State volunteering with SCM.)

THOUSANDS OF REFUGEES FROM AS FAR AWAY AS SOUTH SUDAN and as near to Greece as Syria continue to arrive on the island of Lesvos daily. Their boat landing is just the beginning of their odyssey, which includes both physical travel, as well as negotiating a complex system of rules, laws, and bureaucracy. Once their feet have touched dry ground on Lesvos, they transfer to Moria Camp for food, shelter, and documentation. Here's what it is like for refugees to navigate a day at Moria:

1. You arrive at the camp by bus, taxi or foot. When Moria first opened in the fall of 2015, refugees were walking there from the northern beaches. This could be as far as seventy km. Those who were fortunate enough to retain their belongings when making the sea passage had to carry those belongings and any small children all the way to Moria. Non-governmental agencies (NGO's) are not permitted to transport refugees in their vehicles at all; those caught doing so by authorities risk charges of "trafficking of illegals." Fortunately, the United Nations High Commission for Refugees (UNHCR) is now coordinating bus transportation for refugees who arrive by boat. When you enter at the base of the camp, you are probably wet, exhausted, and emotionally drained.

2. When you disembark the bus, you are separated into two groups (Arabic speakers and others). You line up and receive a numbered wristband. Throughout the day you listen for your number to line up and be registered. Everyone wants to register because without registration papers, you cannot move through Greece or the rest of Europe legally. The registration is in no way a residency permit, but you *must* have it to move on. We have heard stories about Tunisian and Algerian men unable to get registered; they risked arrest and deportation if they left Moria at any time, so they were trapped.

Max. Moria refugee camp, Lesvos, 2016.

3. Either before or after registering, you wander around the camp. If you have energy, you can line up outside any number of temporary "huts" for free tea, dry clothing, etc. Food is only served three times per day. Everywhere you turn, you see families or large groups of people sitting or lying on blankets awaiting something.

4. All those in Moria must exit their sleeping barracks at 8:00 am every day. Those who are registered are free to move both in and outside the camp if they choose. International volunteers and paid Greek cleaning staff thoroughly clean and reorganize the barracks in anticipation of the 3:00 pm re-housing.

5. At 2:30 pm, you and your family join a line that snakes down the hill and waxes and wanes over the next two hours as re-housing takes place. If you are a single man traveling without a wife and/or children, you cannot be housed in the family barracks, even if you are traveling with an extended family. You will be housed in separate barracks or tents.

6. At 3:00 pm, you are welcomed into the housing units, one family at a time, by the volunteer crew, who must figure out the complicated system of trying to house language and ethnic groups together, while separating registered from non-registered refugees. You will end up in a room full of bunks and floor mats where twenty-five to fifty refugees will sleep under UNHCR-issued thick gray blankets.

7. Dinner is served at 7:30 pm in the barracks. Breakfast, lunch, and dinner are free and are generally something resembling rice and vegetables, or curry.

© Anjo Kan / Shutterstock

Two sisters care for their brother. Moria refugee camp, Lesvos, 2016.

8. You can then fall asleep exhausted if you haven't slept through the afternoon and evening.

9. Some Syrian families have the option of being removed from Moria and sent to a satellite camp, Kara Tepe, where they remain until they can come up with Athens ferry fare ($50/adult, under five years free). For these refugees, the move to Kara Tepe is generally a positive step.

10. Repeat steps three through nine every day until you depart Moria Camp. This can take one day to over a week. Limiting factors include registration status, money for tickets to the Greek Mainland and ferry passenger capacity.

If registered refugees are not satisfied with the conditions inside Moria camp, there are other options: One option is staying in a Mytilene hotel for the few who can afford that option. Another option is the outer camp located immediately adjacent to Moria and completely run by volunteers—not the Greek government. It is known as "Better Days for Moria". There, families are offered tents that become their personal space but with less infrastructure.

A long journey is made longer with endless lines, waiting and exhaustion.

7
Bottleneck at Idomeni

March 11, 2016
Idomeni, Greece
Bill Dienst, MD

THE BORDER AT THE SMALL FARMING VILLAGE OF IDOMENI, population 154, between Greece and Macedonia, was sealed with a barbwire fence about four weeks ago. Meanwhile, the refugee population has exploded immediately and exponentially. A few weeks ago, there were fewer than five thousand people living in tents, and they fully expected to pass through. Today there are over fifteen thousand refugees according to official estimates; but if we include refugees living in the "gas station camps" of Eko, BP, and Hara, the number hovers at around twenty thousand desperate people aspiring for a better future free from poverty and war. The future for these people is totally uncertain at this point.

Three days ago, about 500 refugees were allowed to cross into the Republic of Macedonia on their way to Serbia, Slovenia, Austria and ultimately Germany or other locations in northern Europe. The number of people allowed passage is markedly diminished from the thousands that were crossing daily before. Today, that number is zero. On March 8th, the border was completely sealed for refugees. The EU is putting pressure on Turkey to stem the flow of refugees crossing into the Greek Islands too. So now refugees are being stranded in both Turkey and Greece.

According to sources we interviewed here in Idomeni, members of the Greek Army and Police arrived three days ago and blocked the highway heading north to the Macedonian border. Afghans were forced out of the area back to Athens and other unknown destinations.

Based on a walk-through visit of the Idomeni camps yesterday, we see that the majority of refugees remaining now are Syrians, with a minority from other countries. Current UNHCR reports are that about 60% of the refugees remaining in Idomeni are Syrians. The remaining 40% are split among other ethnicities such as Iraqis, Iranians, Pakistanis, Afghans, Moroccans, etc. Sixty Three percent of the current population is comprised of women and children.

According to Spanish journalist Juan Naza who works for a Russian news agency and who has been in the Idomeni area for ten days, there is a general lack of information among the refugees. Some have been stranded here for over three weeks and the majority does not know what to believe or what to do. Some have the ability to search the internet, but many don't even know how to go about consulting the UN about how to proceed.

Medecins San Frontieres (MSF) has erected eight giant tents that shelter about 250 refugees each. UNHCR is deploying additional tents for families, and about half the remaining refugees are in individual tents scattered haphazardly in different makeshift zones now designated as Areas A, B, C, D, and E. The smaller tents erected by families often do not have fly covers, so the rain soaks through. It has been just a few degrees above freezing and raining very hard for the past few days. So everyone is getting thoroughly cold, muddy, and drenched. Many people don't have tents at all. The railway station at Idomeni is no longer functioning. Trains are being by-passed around Idomeni. Its platform, relatively dry ground, has become completely covered with tents and temporary shelters. The snack bars are still functioning, currently chock full of people trying to stay dry.

UNHCR and MSF have erected feeding tents. People cue for over an hour to receive a sandwich, an orange, and water. For many, this is the only meal that they receive for the day. Some other volunteer organizations are providing additional hot meals as well. Limitations in food supplies here are being burdened by rapid expansion in demand, and the fact that MSF and UNHCR are also facing multiple refugee crises around the world, where people also must be fed. Some refugee populations, like in Sudan, are bigger than here. The EU is also trying to provide additional funds, but that demands a political process between the Left and the Right. In Greece, the far-right parties are saying things like, "All of Greece will become like Idomeni if we allow this to go on." MSF has erected portable toilets and showers, but the showers only run cold water, so many people are going without bathing, and hygiene is suffering. Large portions of the population are suffering from upper respiratory infections.

The Greek government has also deployed security police, but they too are feeling overwhelmed with about 40-50 officers for twenty thousand refugees.

There are now moves by the Greek Government to set up reception centers along the lines of what we witnessed at Moria and Tara Kepe camps in Lesvos. The advantage of these reception centers, often placed on military bases, is that there is order and some hygiene measures can be better implemented. But this comes at a loss of personal autonomy for the refugees. And many of these reception centers are located in the middle of nowhere. Some refugees are grudgingly returning to Athens, at a cost of thirty-five Euros each for bus tickets.

German Chancellor Angela Merkel is now saying that it is a mistake to close the Balkan route to northern Europe. But solutions to this humanitarian crisis remain murky.

© Abdulazez Dukhan

A young refugee holds her artwork depicting the military camps in Northern Greece.

8
Predicaments

March 14, 2016
Molyvos
Bill Dienst, MD

Aᴰᴱᴿ ʙᴇɪɴɢ ᴘᴀʀᴛ ᴏꜰ ᴀɴ ᴀᴅᴠᴀɴᴄᴇ ᴛᴇᴀᴍ sent to the Greek-Macedonian border this past week to scope out the situation of twenty thousand refugees stranded at the border, we are back in Lesvos for a few days more. Salaam Cultural Museum is now planning to deploy most of its resources to the border at Idomeni.

The situation here on the north end of Lesvos has cooled down. The Turkish Coast Guard and NATO Naval forces have effectively cut off refugee boat crossings in Zone 1 where we have been assigned. There are still significant numbers of crossings on the south part of the Island near Mytilene, but they are currently well staffed with medical and humanitarian volunteers there. So we will be moving some of our medical operations to the Greek Mainland, to where we can now be put to better use.

Today, I will take this time to reflect on information we received last week from the United Nations High Commission on Refugees (UNHCR).

Boat arrivals to Lesvos have been down. On March 8th, they had declined 20% from the daily average of 1500 arrivals per day recorded the previous week. In spite of this, the populations in Moria and Tara Kepe Camps near Mytilene are still growing, mainly due to a slowdown of refugees leaving for the Greek Mainland. The 4000 capacity in these camps is being built-up to house a population of 6500.

Tickets for refugees to get to Athens and beyond are now being rationed. There are reports of tickets being scalped and sold at highly inflated rates. There are also reports of fraudulent counterfeit tickets being sold, which have no value; and some are claiming direct ferry passage to Idomeni. The only problem is that Idomeni is inland from the sea by more than fifty kilometers and no ferry can get there. But refugees who fall for these fraudulent sales do not know that, and more of their remaining meager funds are being squandered on these rip-offs.

UNHCR believes that if the capacity at Moria Camp exceeds the 6500 currently allocated, more ferry tickets will become available and ferry traffic for refugees will be increased, with ticket sales acting as a "spigot" to allow any overflow in refugee populations to go to Athens.

Meanwhile there are negotiations and proposals between the EU and Turkey to have refugees sent back to Turkey. An agreement on this is pending in the next few days.

There are multiple social problems affecting the refugees, which have now become apparent. First of all, is the problem of separated families. In many cases, the father of a household left several months ago, arrived in northern Europe, became somewhat settled, then called back home to his host country and invited the rest of his family to come. So the wife, children, and sometimes the elders set off and, after a long ordeal, make it to Turkey or Greece, only to be stranded halfway between their relatives back home and their husband-breadwinner in northern Europe. We have heard a few tragic stories of family abandonment by the father in Germany in some of these cases.

Then there is the fact that 40% of the current arrivals are children. For many children, there is an absence of a safety net. The ones who are traveling with one or both parents are relatively lucky. There are also children who are traveling only with extended relatives such as aunts, uncles, cousins, etc. Then there are children traveling with no direct relatives at all, perhaps only with neighbors or people who are from their same village. These situations are being dubbed, "extended-extended families."

There are teams of pediatricians and social workers in Greece trying to figure out how to handle children who seem to be on their own. In some cases, children are sent to children's boarding houses in Athens. But these are "open" facilities; that is, these children are free to leave if they choose to do so. This then puts them at risk for predators: human trafficking, sexual enslavement, etc. Children's rights organizations and Europol are now getting involved in efforts to handle this impending tragedy.

9
Ship to Nowhere

Wednesday, March 16, 2016
Aboard the Greek ferry *Nisos Mykonos*, leaving the Port of Mytilene, Lesvos for the Greek mainland.
Bill Dienst, MD

DURING THE LAST DAYS WE SPENT ON THE NORTH SHORE OF LESVOS, we have witnessed, in front of our seaside hotel, the arrival of an armada of NATO naval ships from Germany, Canada, and other countries, which were passing through the straits between Greece and Turkey. There have been fifteen large warships, at least. As far as we can tell, they are probably heading to the south end of the island. We think they are here to help stanch the flow of boat refugees that have still been crossing across the wider straits in the south directly into Mytilene. During the past month, crossings have been very few in our area of operations in the north. The Turkish Coast Guard, under pressure from the EU, has effectively blocked most of the crossings.

So now our NGO, Salaam Cultural Museum is deploying much of our assets to the Greek Mainland in areas of crisis and greater need: specifically to the border village of Idomeni where thousands of refugees are now stranded up against a fence topped with razor wire set up by authorities of the Former Yugoslav Republic of Macedonia (FYROM). This is not to be confused with Macedonia, the region of northern Greece where we are now setting up our operations. We packed up a large van with all the humanitarian and medical supplies that we could possibly stuff into it; and then we headed to the south of Lesvos, an hour's drive over a twisty mountainous road, and into the Port of Mytilene.

The scene at the ferry terminal was poignant: A long cue of Syrian refugees, still with hopes in their hearts for a better future, lined the dock. Finally, they have made it across "the Straits of Death" at $1000 apiece paid to smugglers to get to Lesvos. They spent their time in the transitional camps at Moria or Kara Tepe. Now for about $60 each, they can cross in comfort to Kavala on the Greek Mainland, an eight-hour voyage with beautiful scenery and relatively zero risk of drowning. From there, they will make their way northward.

A Syrian man tells me confidently and triumphantly during our conversation in pidgin Arabic, "I am going to Germany!" Knowing what I now know, I have my doubts about his ability to succeed, but I do not have the heart, nor the Arabic language skills, to warn him about the harrowing trail ahead; so I just let it go. We take pictures of ourselves together as "*habibis*" (good buddies). Another Syrian man tells me his family will stay with friends in Kavala and only head up to the Idomeni if the border opens again. This seems like a much better informed decision.

The Syrians climb up the gangway up to the 6th level and are seated at the stern. They are the lucky ones. They are free to move about most areas of the ship, more or less, though there seems to be a dividing line starboard side aft. Forward from there are the second-class passengers, mostly Greeks and other Westerners, including ourselves. First Class passengers who do not want to deal with the refugee crisis at all are conveniently accommodated in the bow.

On the sixth level portside is a coffee shop, complete with WIFI. Forward from that is a roped off area where we are not allowed to go. But we can see a large contingent of Greek policemen, and what appear to be "prisoners." Some are handcuffed. They are mostly men, but there are a few women too. I suspect these are people, who for one reason or another, were unable to get registered. If these unregistered refugees dare to wander off from the internment camps where they are housed, and they get caught, they risk arrest.

Whether one gets registered or not often has to do with nationality: Syrians and sometimes Iraqis are favored and deemed "war refugees". Afghans, Pakistanis, Moroccans and others are considered "economic refugees" and are less likely to be able to get registered. Of course, the details of each person's individual case are much more complicated than that, as UNHCR has argued. Places like Afghanistan are hardly at peace. But the Greek authorities are doing the best they can, trying to sort things out and restore order in the middle of the chaos of this refugee crisis.

To me, the whole process seems political. The Al-Assad regime and ISIS, though on opposite sides of the spectrum, are both American and western European adversaries. The Shiite dominated Iraqi regime, placed in power after the US invasion and overthrow of Saddam Hussein, are supposedly "our friends." But ISIS exists there too, so both "our friends" and "our enemies" are there. Afghanistan has another regime placed in power following an American and NATO invasion. They are also "our friends," but what about the Taliban? To me all I see in front of me are a lot of worn, tired huddled masses yearning to be free from war and wanting to have a better future for their families. It doesn't seem to matter much beyond that.

Then there is a limitation of incarceration facilities on Lesvos, so I suspect these "prisoners" are headed to more secure facilities on the Greek Mainland. There, they will probably face more accelerated deportation procedures that try to send them back from wherever they came, or else to Turkey. Then they will be Turkey's problem, not Europe's.

Above on the 7th deck, portside forward at midship, there is an overflow of Syrians who are allowed to walk outside on the observation decks. We befriend them, share photo shots, and I do my physical-comedy *shtick* with the children and get them laughing. Behind the Syrians portside aft are another group of people guarded by a smaller contingent of Greek policemen.

They have darker complexions than the Syrians and their manner of dress is different. The police do not allow us to interact with them directly. I think they are Afghans or Pakistanis who are probably not registered. Their trips to the bathroom are monitored so they do not try to slip away and mix anonymously with the Syrians. When we reach landfall, they are probably headed to another internment camp on the mainland until their disposition is decided.

We disembark in our huge van after the ferry arrives at Kavala. We see several large prison-type buses and a lot more Greek policemen waiting to receive the unregistered passengers and prisoners. We drive onward through the night, arriving on the outskirts of the huge encampment of refugees at Idomeni just before midnight.

II
Stranded in Macedonia

10
Desperation and Uncertainty

March 25, 2016
Idomeni Greece, just south of the border with the former Yugoslav Republic
of Macedonia.
Bill Dienst, MD

Since leaving Lesvos, we have spent a little more than a week at Idomeni
on the Greek side of the Macedonian border. The day before we left, I
attended the Tuesday coordination meeting where we were briefed again by a
UNHCR representative. At that point, he predicted that the refugee population on Lesvos would be increasing due to limited accommodations in Athens,
Idomeni and other places. He projected that Lesvos would experience a piling
up of unregistered refugees. Contingency plans to house expanding numbers
of refugees on Lesvos were in the works.

Then three days later, an agreement was signed between the European
Union and Turkey. On the fifth day, the entire refugee populations of Moria
and Tara Keppe camps on Lesvos were abruptly put on buses, driven to the
port, loaded on a giant ferry, and sent to relocation centers on the Greek
mainland, where they await deportation back to Turkey, we think. But we are
not really sure. It is all speculation. But now there are hardly any refugees left
on Lesvos. Elaborate medical and humanitarian operations there, that were
developed following the boat people crisis this past fall and winter, are now
rapidly shutting down.

We really don't know what might happen now on the border here at
Idomeni: not in the short-term; not in the long-term either. Will the population at Idomeni a month from now be at thirty thousand, or will it be zero?
As medical professionals and humanitarians, we must still do our very best to
plan for the future.

The stranded refugee populations here are centered at Idomeni and three
other smaller camps that have grown up around the local gas stations: Eko,
Hara, and BP. Some people have given up and are taking buses back to
Athens. Other people are still arriving. Campsites are spreading out laterally
over wheat fields to reduce clutter and crowding. So it is hard for us to tell

right now if the overall population is contracting or expanding. Smoke billows out from continuous campfires, built for both cooking and for keeping warm. The downside is that we medics are seeing hundreds of people with sore throats, coughs and irritated eyes from chronic smoke exposure, which are also complicating widespread upper respiratory infections. The only respite from this is when it rains, or when the cold winds blow. But then people get muddier and colder.

Our short-term purpose is to provide acute and urgent health care through a mobile health van we have created. We have aligned ourselves with a British group called "Off Track Health." They have a Swedish ambulance that is not operating as such, since that would challenge the existing Greek laws about foreigners running an ambulance. So instead, the back end of this ambulance has been outfitted with various medications and other acute care supplies.

We have modified our existing van in similar fashion. On Lesvos, our van was outfitted with more emergency supplies for treating hypothermia from pulling people off overcrowded boats and out of the water. There was risk for mass casualty incidents, drownings and near drownings. Here, we are handling problems, most of which are not immediately life threatening, but which are directly related to present living conditions and overcrowding: Upper respiratory infections, mostly viral, but some with bacterial complications. Vomiting, diarrhea, and the like are also being seen. We are also screening for more serious conditions, and devising elaborate ways to send people needing hospital care an hour away to the local hospital in the town of Kilkis. When necessary, we manage emergency conditions as best we can and wait for the Greek ambulance to arrive.

Every day is a new adventure, as we do our very best to make order out of chaos. We start out at the "medical supply warehouse", which is really a musty basement where we store donations from around the world. A few days ago, we had to sort through piles of boxes and suitcases full of stuff, some things that are useful to us and some things that are not. But thanks to a group of German medical students who spent two whole days building shelves and sorting meds into alphabetical order by drug name and by category, we can now find what we have and need in a fraction of the time.

Our medications are in English, German and in Greek. There are also some differences between the USA and Europe: e.g. Acetaminophen (Tylenol) is Paracetamol here. Even when we can figure out the generic ingredients in German and in Greek, we often discover that our European colleagues use some different preparations for cough and cold that we have never heard of in the States.

We have different groups of doctors, nurses and other allied health professionals every day, as many of our volunteers stay with us in northern Greece for a week or so, and then return home to their own countries. During the past week, I have worked shoulder to shoulder with health care providers from the UK, Ireland, Norway, Sweden, Germany, Switzerland, Austria, and Catalonia, The cooperation and collegiality that I have experienced working alongside these wonderful brothers and sisters has been inspiring and amazing!

We line up our mobile health van on the edge of camp with special considerations for crowd control. We try our best to get people to cue up in two lines. We send people trying to cut into the line back to the end. We have an intake person who pairs with a translator (mostly Arabic, but also Kurdish, Urdu, and Pashtu). When we are limited by the number of translators, we employ local people who speak some English to help with translation so that the lines don't get too long. Then each patient is seen by a doctor working through the translator. After evaluating the patient, the doctor requests medications from a makeshift "trained on the spot" gofer/pharmacy technician who does her very best to keep order in the van. We typically see about 100 patients among three doctors in a three-hour period in this way. Our notations are brief: Patient age, sex, assessment, and treatment. We try our best to get specific names if we think follow up or specialty care is needed.

Yesterday, I attended a general medical meeting with the medical director of Medecins San Frontieres (Doctors Without Borders) and the heads of some of the twenty plus NGO's who are providing health care here in Idomeni. The purpose of this weekly meeting is to do strategic planning and coordination of medical services for the long term, even though we cannot know what the long term will look like. In the next article, I will try to explain what some of the longer-term goals are. Our targets keep moving and evolving.

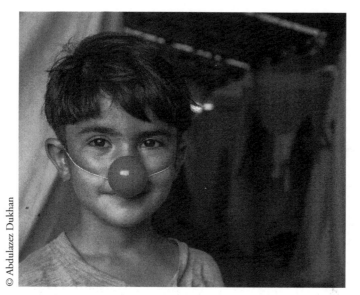

© Abdulazez Dukhan

A refugee child plays with a nose left behind by entertainers from Clowns Without Borders.

11
Order From Chaos

April 1, 2016
Idomeni
Bill Dienst, MD

A WEEK LATER, SEVERAL CHANGES are apparent here on the Greek-Macedonian border. The refugee population at Idomeni is starting to be reduced, slightly. Last Saturday, we witnessed a convoy of four buses full of refugees heading south on the Highway with police escorts. As far as we can tell, it appears that the population, once estimated as high as twenty thousand, is diminishing by several hundred each day.

We are hearing that these are refugees who are willing to leave voluntarily: i.e. those who have had enough. These people are heading to reception or relocation centers, which are being set up by the Greek military on the Greek Mainland. There, the hope is that they will have better living conditions and three square meals a day in exchange for finally sacrificing their ambitions to cross into the Balkan republics, and onward to northern Europe.

Still, many thousands remain, who, so far, will not leave voluntarily. These are people who have invested all of their physical and financial resources to get this far and still have hopes, albeit fading, for pressing on to Germany. Tensions are mounting. This past Sunday, the refugees who remain were joined by Italian and Spanish activists who flew in for the weekend to show their solidarity. They all assembled Sunday morning on the railroad tracks in the center of the refugee camp, about a hundred meters from the border. There, they were met by hundreds of Greek riot police, and a face-to-face standoff ensued.

Salaam Cultural Museum was trying to enter Idomeni camp with our mobile health van. We were blocked by the Greek Police while getting off the highway. We had to double back and take a forty km detour through back roads and beautiful countryside of foothills and vineyards to get to the camp. As we approached the camp, I jumped out with some others at the railway station and walked up the tracks through areas B and A toward Area C, while our van negotiated the traffic to get into position at our usual spot.

We crossed the tracks in the middle of the confrontation, tense but not yet violent. A large crowd of refugees and their Italian and Spanish allies stood face to face with a line of police in full riot gear and shields. Slogans were being shouted. Our Norwegian partners, Medics Bergen were on standby with their trauma packs in hand. We pressed on 300 meters and met up with our mobile health van in our usual spot in Area C across the road from the cluster of tents, which have become known as "Little Kurdistan". There are also districts of Idomeni populated by Arabic speaking Syrians, Iraqis, and Yazidis as well as Pakistanis and Afghans who speak Urdu, Pashtu, and Dari. There are other nationalities as well. Sometimes there are tensions and fights between these different ethnic groups.

As we arrive, there does not seem to be much happening in terms of primary care at our usual spot. Many people are heading in the opposite direction toward the tracks and the border with all their belongings, and with hopes they might finally get across. I start pulling our trauma first aid packs from the van and handing them out to our volunteers, with the intention of sending them back toward the tracks. But wait a minute . . . here is a Syrian family wanting some primary care. So we decide to see them before heading to the tracks. But before we can finish, several others arrive. And not too long after that, a long line assembles and we are back in business. Hours later, we see the Greek riot police walking out peacefully. Conflict has somehow been avoided, but I am not certain about the details. I have been caught up examining a lot of people with coughs, sore throats, and other maladies.

So that was Sunday. On Monday, I inherit the role of being medical director of a freestanding medical clinic, which was constructed out of plywood and tarp by Medecins sans Frontieres. MSF decided to consolidate their operations in Idomeni. So they have handed over operations for the clinic at Eko gas station to us. We move in on Monday. We outfit the clinic that morning, and start seeing patients at 2:00 pm. We have now offered thirteen hours of continuous patient service per day for the past two days. Now it is Thursday.

Salaam Cultural Museum and Off Track Health had previously been present during the past few weeks running mobile health clinics at Eko gas station. Previously, Eko was the last bus stop where passengers coming from Athens were let off. Refugees getting off the bus there then had the option of taking a taxi, or walking twenty km up the highway to the border at Idomeni, or pitching a tent right there at Eko. And so many tents sprung up there, including several large ones sponsored by UNHCR. Now, a community of perhaps 2,000 refugees exists. It's a ready-made small town of refugees for this small town doctor, now medical director of this small town clinic, with a very small medical staff that changes every week.

12
Hearts, Souls & Minds

April 4, 2016
EKO Gas Station Refugee Camp, Highway 75 near Polykastro, Greece.
Bill Dienst, MD

"If you are in your twenties and you aren't a bit of a revolutionary, you have no heart. But if you are in your 50's and do not have some conservative tendencies, you have no brain."
(Improvising on a quote that has been falsely attributed to Winston Churchill, but still makes sense to me.)

OUR MAKESHIFT TOWN OF REFUGEE TENTS cluttered around the Eko gas station is on the highway, two kilometers south of the exit to Polykastro, Greece. It has mostly Syrian refugees who speak Arabic and Kurdish. The current estimated population here is about 2,200 people. Last Monday, our coalition of small NGO's inherited a small plywood building, which serves as a primary care clinic from Medecins sans Frontieres. MSF wanted to consolidate their operations among the much larger refugee populations in Idomeni, which are located twenty km to the north, immediately adjacent to the Macedonian border. People have been stranded there for over a month, trying to take the Balkan route to northern Europe.

Our refugees at Eko are stranded too. For this small town family/ER doctor and my committed colleagues of doctors, family nurse practitioners, nurses, emergency medical technicians and other humanitarians from all around the world, it has been an intense labor of love this past week getting this clinic stocked with medications, bandages, tools, and other supplies. We have even bought a refrigerator so we can handle perishables, including vaccinations, which we hope may be coming to us through MSF in the near future. Immediately, we begin staffing the clinic thirteen hours per day with three shifts of intake people, doctors, nurses, and translators. Things are going well, and every day, the chaos is slowly but surely becoming more manageable.

Previously, we were providing primary health care out of the back end of mobile health vans. We still do this in Idomeni. But in these settings, it is extremely difficult to do much about chronic conditions like hypertension, diabetes, epilepsy, and the like. Now for the first time, we are beginning to make progress in managing these chronic conditions. We are also beginning to make in-roads and relationships with Greek doctors at the Polykastro Health Center, so we can line up lab, X-ray, and dental services. The local Greek doctors and all of us realize that we must be allies in health care. They need us to take the pressure off them with the overwhelming medical needs that this refugee crisis has created; and we need them to help us with ER, lab, X ray, and dental services that we are yet unable to provide. We have accomplished a lot in just one short week.

Then on Friday and Saturday, the bottom drops out. It all starts when Greek government officials show up Friday morning asking for credentials for our doctors and nurses; this is problematic, since our medical staff is comprised of volunteer health professionals from all over Europe, North America, and Asia. Many of our health staff arrive, work intensely for one or two weeks and then return to their home countries. But we do our best to comply with these new onerous requirements. We send a team Friday night an hour south to the city of Thessaloniki to meet with government officials. When our team returns, we think we have a workable plan to assemble credentials within the following few days to keep our clinic operational. Mairi Calder, our Scottish logistics coordinator works feverishly through the night putting dossiers together for each of our providers, even those scheduled to leave in just a few days.

On Saturday morning, three more government officials arrive, demanding our paperwork immediately. They seem irritated and then they leave. An hour later they return with the police. Under duress, we are forced to shut our clinic down in the middle of a very busy Saturday. The refugees protest by blocking the highway with their tents; passenger vehicles are allowed to pass, but all commercial trucking is blocked. The situation becomes more volatile and more police reinforcements arrive.

This is a heart-wrenching experience for both our Syrian patients and us providers. We have quickly grown quite close each other in our makeshift small town. We are starting to know the names of the people and their families; and they are starting to know us.

What each of us thinks should be done about this mess varies depending on who we are, how old we are and how long we are volunteering with refugee health care. I feel that I must pace myself and pick my battles; only the ones I think I have a chance of winning. At age fifty-seven, I can no longer be Don Quixote chasing windmills, I simply don't have the stamina. As medical coordinator, I am trying my best to work smarter, so that someday soon all of us will not have to work so hard struggling with the latest crisis of the hour. This does not mean that I don't care. It is all a matter of tactics.

There are some who think this is all a deliberate attempt by the Greek government to make life in these makeshift camps so miserable that more refugees will go willingly to the relocation centers based on the military bases. There, the hope is that they will have better conditions and more consistent health care from Greek military doctors and the German Red Cross. Honestly, I feel ambivalent about this whole process. If refugees are all going to be forced into these relocation centers sooner or later, isn't it better that it happens sooner? There are no easy answers.

But now I sometimes feel that I am at loggerheads with one young EMT, with a revolutionary bent, who I fear might have intent toward confronting the Greek authorities. We have to keep talking him down. He is in his 20's, emotionally shattered, and hasn't had a day off in weeks. He won't take a day off and he really should. He is showing the telltale signs of burning out. I know them well, for I have been there many times in my career myself. It is not whether or not you will burn out doing this kind of humanitarian work; you will. It is only a matter of time. What is more important is whether or not you will recover from your burnout and remain resilient and compassionate. His heart tells him that he must act.

I am trying to use my brain while acknowledging to the younger ones in our medical corps that I too still have a heart, even if my distancing from every crisis of the hour doesn't make it seem so to them. I do still care. I will never resort to pure pragmatic *real-politik* and opportunism, like all the scoundrels that have created this horrific modern day catastrophe in the Middle East: Bush, Netanyahu, Al-Assad, the Saudi regime and many others, including those who have profited from endless wars. For every outrageous action, there are equally outrageous reactions: so now we have ISIS, among others.

When will it stop? I do not know. All I can do is to try to help the vulnerable and the meek. I must ask myself, "How can I help?" Easy question, the answers are not always so easy. The corollary to this is, "If you are going to be a rescuer, do not become a casualty, not physically nor emotionally."

It was bound to happen and one day it did. With all the hundreds of sick people coughing in our faces every day, I and others have picked up the nasty upper respiratory illness going around, compounded by all the dust and smoke in our working environment. In my case, even in spite of having gotten my flu shot . . . so now we are all becoming wounded healers too.

We must work with the Greek authorities and jump through whatever hoops they ask of us, as best we can. After all, we are in their country and we will never win by provoking them. The predicament that they are in deserves sympathy too.

Our best response is to develop alliances with all the parties. The director of the Polykastro Health Center, Dr Georgios Perperidis is also a dentist. He is a very important man to know. He also knows all the local officials in the Greek Ministry of Health and says he will advocate with them on our behalf. On Sunday, we all meet with Dr Jolien Colpaert who is the medical coordinator with MSF. We work out an elaborate plan to keep the Eko Clinic going under an alliance of small NGO's.

We all show up Monday morning to finalize the deal only to discover that two of the critical NGOs refuse to collaborate with each other, based on bad blood between them in the past. A lot is lost in translation. Dr Perperidis explains in Greek that all the problems with the Greek Government officials have been resolved adequately. However, it is still a no-go due to what seems to me to be petty differences between rival NGO's. Who are we working for again? The Refugees!

MSF now needs to take the clinic back for the next week or so, even though they don't want to. The clinic sits dormant and padlocked for several days while we all work out of mobile health vans again. Our clinic needs to be disassembled due to competing assets and competing interests. We have wasted a lot of effort trying to build this dream. We can no longer blame it all on the Greeks. We seem to have become our own worst enemy.

Are you feeling exhausted, humiliated, and sick; a little burned out perhaps? You bet I am!

OK, step back, slow down. Take care of yourself. It's not just a destination, it is an adventure. Go back to running mobile clinics now, and see where all this goes.

13
Rumors

Sunday April 10, 2016
Idomeni
Bill Dienst, MD

Iᴛ's 8:00 ᴀᴍ. I arrive at breakfast in our *Hotel Maison*, located forty minutes south of the Greek-Macedonian border where thousands of Syrian and other refugees remain stranded. David Stanton, the EMT working for Medics Bergen tells me about rumors he has heard the night before: large numbers of refugees are planning to breach the border today. I have heard similar rumors in the past from time to time, but nothing much has happened so far on my watch.

Two weeks ago, also on Sunday, there was a big standoff between the refugees, encouraged by Spanish and Italian solidarity activists, and the Greek Police clad in full riot gear on the railroad tracks, one-hundred meters from the fence. We had our trauma bags deployed, fully ready, but the situation eased off several hours later. As far as I know, no one was hurt. The activists went back to Italy and Spain the next day, and the refugees went back to their squalor and their tents. We went back to treating colds and sore throats. Several hundred refugees boarded buses and left Idomeni for "relocation centers," while thousands of others still remain. People are becoming more stir-crazy and reckless. Children walk aimlessly right in front of my car, and I must drive extremely defensively in order not to hit them by mistake.

I head north to Eko Gas Station refugee camp and attend the weekly medical logistics meeting for our coalition of small NGO's. My medical and humanitarian team goes directly to the medical warehouse in Polykastro to restock our mobile health van. We stock up every morning to prepare first for our mid-day clinic at Idomeni, and then our evening clinic back at Eko. While at the morning Eko meeting, I hear more substantial rumors that several hundred refugees left Eko at 6:00 am this morning and are presently walking twenty km to the border at Idomeni: They are going to try to cross. Many left with their belongings in tow, just in case they get the chance.

We finish our meeting at about 11:00 am. After the meeting I head north to join my colleagues to start our clinic in our usual spot in Area C at Idomeni. When I arrive, I see thousands of people, not just at the usual spot of protest at the railroad tracks, but to the west right smack-dab up against the fence topped with concertina wire; and some are trying to cut their way through.

On the immediate opposite side of the fence are riot police and soldiers from the Former Yugoslav Republic of Macedonia (FYROM). Tanks with mounted machine guns and Armored Personnel Vehicles (APV's) are there too. Things escalate; rocks are thrown across the fence at the soldiers, and FYROM forces respond with tear gas and sound grenades.

As I approach our Mobile Health Van located 250 meters south of the fence, I see David the EMT stumbling back, extremely sweaty, clammy, and coughing uncontrollably. He has been tear-gassed. We douse him with water, and he starts to recover. Moments later, we start receiving dozens more who have received more intense gas exposures. We start shifting into Mass Casualty Incident mode.

As we get over our initial astonishment and emotional shock, we start to get a handle on the situation. We start triaging people based on intensity of symptoms and associated trauma, related directly to the melee. Chaos and pandemonium dominate, and now we need to exert crowd control measures. We instruct our translators to start shouting loudly in Arabic, "Family members only! All others who are not hurt need to back away!"

Some people have been struck with billy clubs or rubber bullets, but 90% are simply suffering from different levels of tear gas inhalation. A few are splinted for possible fractures and we call the Greek Ambulance for one suspected low back/pelvic fracture. We send some of our volunteers forward wearing masks and equipped with one-liter water bottles with a hole punched into the middle of the cap, so they can quickly douse those gassed in the face and mitigate the severity of their symptoms, thus reducing their need to be carried by others to our van. Most of these cases are self-limiting. One man gets IM epinephrine as we are concerned about his impending respiratory collapse, and several with asthmatic reactions receive bronchodilator therapy.

The wind suddenly shifts to the south, and all of us medical volunteers are now being gassed too. We again become wounded healers. Our van pulls back one hundred meters further south through trampled wheat fields to try and escape the gas. The Swedish ambulance mobile health van becomes trapped when its tire gets stuck in a muddy trough in the wheat field, and we have to assemble a team of strong men to free it up.

This immediately feels familiar to me: instant recall. A feeling one never forgets if you have been tear-gassed before: the burning on your face, the intense watering and stinging of your eyes; the uncontrollable sneezing and coughing. The feeling that you are going to suffocate, and then it passes, just as long as you don't die right away: two minutes, five minutes, ten minutes, depending on the concentration of gas you received and any pre-morbid conditions you might also have.

It has been ten years since my previous and only other gassing. This one occurred in 2006 at the hands of Israeli Occupation Forces in the West Bank village of Bil'in. There, those weekly gas attacks continue to this day. They involve concertina wire fences too, built to steal valuable olive groves from Palestinian villages and incorporate them into Jewish-only settlements. The tools used there and here are the same: concussion grenades, tear gas, rubber coated steel bullets, and sometimes live ammunition. For me, that gas attack back then was much worse than this one; compounded by a concussion grenade that exploded right next to me and left my ears ringing for hours.

The FYROM forces are now using rubber bullets and I am hoping it goes no further. We have previously seen a Greek helicopter, but now a FYROM military helicopter approaches, weaves in and out, then hovers menacingly over the border. I again start having quivering flashbacks having seen American-supplied Apache attack helicopters in Gaza before firing heavy shells over our heads from the sky and killing young men behind us. I am praying that it will not come to this.

I am sure leaders from both Greece and Macedonia do not want any further escalation either. The last thing either country needs right now is a war provoked by this current refugee crisis, given that the economies of both countries have been in the tank, even before all this.

We think the gas victims are waning, but they continue coming in waves. Gradually, the numbers keep getting smaller. It's three o'clock in the afternoon. We pack up our van and head to Polykastro for lunch.

© Bill Dienst

Riot police block off the train tracks leading north through the Balkans in Idomeni, a small village on the Greece/Macedonia border.

14
Vincent's Story

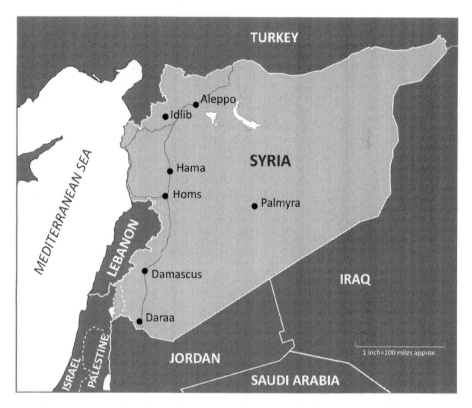

April 12, 2016
Eko Gas Station Camp
Bill Dienst, MD

VINCENT (NOT HIS REAL NAME) IS A FRIEND OF MINE. He is a 28-year-old man from Syria with a warped sense of humor. He acts like a child because he never had a childhood. He volunteers every day with our mobile healthcare van serving as one of our Arabic-English translators.

He greets me every day, shouting and laughing, "Kill Bill!" I must admit,

I find this unnerving. He goes on and on about these Quentin Tarantino movies, which I have yet to see. He thinks they are fabulous! "Just like a cartoon," he exclaims.

I am trying to use him to help me do patient interviews. The line of patients keeps getting longer and longer. I am trying to focus on patient care. Vincent keeps trying to tell his jokes. Many I find foul-mouthed and disgusting. I won't even try to repeat them here. The line keeps getting longer and I find myself getting frustrated. Frankly, I find him obnoxious at this point. I am starting to resent that I am stuck with him.

Then something happens, which changes my initial impressions. Late at night as the Eko clinic is winding down, we are evaluating sick nine-month-old dehydrated child who has had continuous diarrhea for eight days. This child needs to be hospitalized, and the closest hospital is in the Greek town of Kilkis, over forty km away, across farm fields in the dark.

The main problem facing us now is lack of transportation. This child is not sick enough to warrant an ambulance, which is hard to come by anyway. I also need an Arabic-English translator to help the Greek doctor at the hospital.

So I go with this child, his mother and Vincent in my small Hertz rental car all the way to Kilkis (population about sixty thousand): three Syrians and one American. None of us has ever been to Kilkis before. I am glad I have studied the Greek alphabet, so I can read road signs and not get too lost trying to get to the hospital.

I wince at the idea of having to listen to Vincent's warped sense of humor all the way to Kilkis. I start by asking him what he thinks should be done to resolve the crisis in Syria. "Drop a huge nuclear bomb on the whole country!" I ask him why? "Then all the people who are suffering and dying slowly will finally be put out of their misery!"

Then a funny thing happens. A tormented soul emerges from his internal angst, stops all the sick jokes, and starts telling me his personal story.

Vincent was not born not in Syria, but in Iraq. This is because his grandfather was a political opponent of former Syrian President Hafez Al-Assad, the current President Bashar's father. Vincent's family fled to Iraq to avoid persecution. His father divorced his mother when he was about three years old, so he never really knew his father. His mother suffered severe post-partum depression after the birth of younger brother Mohammed. His mother killed his younger brother by cutting his head off. This also happened when young Vincent was still only three. His mother has been mentally disturbed ever since, and Vincent has distanced himself from her.

As a result of all this turmoil, Vincent was raised by his grandmother, with whom he is now closest. In 1995, when he was seven years old, the family returned to Syria while trying to escape the growing hardships resulting from the American orchestrated attacks on Iraq, followed by the no-fly zones and the embargo.

Upon returning to Syria, the entire family was immediately arrested, and Vincent became a seven-year-old prisoner. "For me, prison was like a school," he says. There were fellow prisoners who served as teachers. After three months, the family was released, albeit with multiple restrictions: no passports and no educational opportunities. He and his family also suffered from social isolation because friends and acquaintances risked persecution for any association with his family. They were not allowed to rent a flat, etc. Over time, the restrictions eased somewhat after the second American invasion of Iraq in 2003. Vincent was able to finish high school and enter the University at Latakia in 2009. "Those were the best three years of my life," he laments nostalgically.

Then the Arab Spring happened in 2011. Initial circumstances seemed optimistic and encouraging, especially after apparent progress in Tunisia and Egypt. But then, the Al-Assad regime put down an iron fist. Many of Vincent's friends, neighbors, and their entire families were slaughtered. Fellow students and friends were gunned down in the streets by snipers. Vincent continued in school for another year, but then conditions became too oppressive, so he had to leave the University and flee for his life, having finished only three of his four years. He almost earned a degree in English literature, which is why he can now serve as one of our translators.

He went back to his hometown and his family, and also to hideout from security forces who wanted him to serve in the Syrian Army. He hid out within the confines of his home in his small town for three years, afraid to show his face outside: no job, no life, no income, no friends, etc.

Then family members with money offered him the financial means to take the chance to escape all this madness and go to Turkey. And so he set off.

To get to Turkey, he had to cross Syrian territory that was occupied by DA'ISH (ISIS). Unfortunately, he was captured, tortured, and imprisoned for two months. Some of the torture he experienced included ten days of sleep deprivation, being hung by his wrists suspended in the air for hours on end, being bludgeoned, being subjected to electric shocks, and being threatened with knives, gasoline, and fire. He was asked to recite verses from the Koran, and fortunately, he was able to do so, sufficiently. This probably saved his life, as he saw friends and comrades who had their necks slashed to death because they could not.

ISIS finally moved on to other torture victims and released him. Pressing onward to the Turkish border in the dark, he had to traverse minefields and ISIS night patrols with mounted machine guns chasing and killing those behind him.

He made it across the border into Turkey. He then paid smugglers over a thousand dollars to bring him overland to Istanbul, and then onward to Izmir. He paid other smugglers an additional thousand dollars to take a harrowing rubber dinghy overfilled with refugees across the straits to the Greek Island of Chios. There he registered with the Greek government, received a six-month visa and made it by ferry to Athens and the Greek Mainland. After thirteen days touring Athens, he took a train to Thessaloniki, and then a bus, which dropped him off at Eko gas station where he joined his "homies" (friends) in a tent. This is where he is now stranded. So with not much else to do, he is helping us take care of other Syrians who are sick.

Vincent has now given up on any illusions about reaching Germany. His current hope is that he can somehow integrate himself here in Greece. Given what I now know, I see that it is better to have a warped sense of humor than no sense of humor at all.

> Now I understand what you tried to say to me
> How you suffered for your sanity
> How you tried to set them free.
> They would not listen
> They did not know how
> Perhaps they'll listen now[1]

---

1. From "Starry Starry Night," Don McLean's ballad about Vincent Van Gogh, 1972.

15
Confrontation & Suppression

Monday-Wednesday April 11-13, 2016
Idomeni
Bill Dienst, MD

O<small>N</small> M<small>ONDAY,</small> <small>WE</small> <small>EXPERIENCED</small> <small>THE</small> <small>AFTERMATH</small> of processing our own emotions, those which we had no time to digest while it was all happening on Sunday: the tear gas, the sound bombs, the rubber bullets, the stampeding people full of panic, and the adrenaline rush of it all. The morning after brings with it a hangover of somber moods, as we reflect on what it all means: the growing loss of any hope among the lingering refugees.

I have been through all these emotions before in Gaza.[2] First, there is an oddly euphoric feeling of being alive during all the excitement of being under attack, then melancholy; and then feeling depressed with Post Traumatic Stress symptoms later.

But we have no time for all that now. We must get out of bed, have breakfast, and head back to the front at Idomeni. With some trepidation, we proceed with our mobile health van, and set up in our usual spot.

Monday turns out to be fairly routine. We are back to our usual practice-pattern of "Urgent Care, Light." Our practice here mainly consists of lot of self-limiting conditions for which we can only provide symptomatic relief. We also see a lot of chronic complex medical and social problems, which we can do little about because we have yet to build up sufficient infrastructure. There are also the few cases where antibiotics are indicated. We provide a few wound dressings for second-degree burns from hot water and campfires.

It's the usual stuff, seemingly boring, but showing the people that we still care for them while they are feeling that most of the world has forgotten them and their current predicament. We practice the art of primary care medicine: First Do No harm! Try your best not to over-medicate those with emotional distress, which keep coming back to us with physical complaints. But we must also concentrate and try not to miss those few serious conditions that require our medical intervention either.

Tuesday is much like Monday. Our mobile clinic at Idomeni runs smoothly, and I end my day there with the usual coordination meeting with Medecins sans Frontieres, Medecins du Monde, and the heads from all the other smaller NGO's like us, who are providing health care in the camps. We review our response to Mass Casualty Incidents, like the one that occurred on Sunday, and how we can collaborate better. We hear that three people with asthma died of respiratory failure as a complication of the tear gas over in Area A.

We are trying to start a vaccination program, but are still awaiting a green light from the Greek government. There is a clinical report of a case of measles without lab confirmation. We fear preventable epidemics might break out at any time given the huge numbers of unvaccinated children living in close quarters.

Then when we least expect it, Wednesday turns out to be a much different day. When we arrive, refugees are again amassing at the fence, and a standoff with Macedonian troops on the other side is already underway. There are fewer protesters this time than there were on Sunday. A few tear gas canisters and sound grenades fly. Then from the west, we see a column of Greek riot police moving forward to the east, fully equipped with riot shields and billy clubs, creating a wedge between the refugee protesters and the fence, with the FYROM soldiers watching from the other side.

Greece and Macedonia (or FYROM, as the Greeks prefer to call it) have had their share of hostilities in the recent and distant past. But neither side is looking for an armed conflict. The economies of both countries are suffering, even before this refugee crisis began. The last thing either country needs right now is a war provoked by this refugee crisis. This escalation could easily have happened last Sunday, especially when the FYROM helicopter weaved menacingly along the border. I am sure it was equipped with attack weapons, which could have been unleashed into the crowd below.

On Monday, the media was full of reports from the Greek government, which were critical of how the FYROM government handled the situation. But nobody in either government wants any further escalation. The Greek riot forces are now advancing their wedge, to cleave the refugees away from the fence. People are struck with billy clubs, and we start taking casualties at our mobile health van.

We get fewer tear gas injuries compared to Sunday, but more lacerations courtesy of the Greek riot police, about five cases within just a few minutes. Fortunately we are equipped with staple guns, which are much quicker than using conventional sutures. We have no time to dilly-dally. We must work fast, because we don't know when the deluge of patients will stop. First iodine to disinfect, then wash the wound with saline, then lidocaine injection, then staples: pop, pop, pop! Antibiotic ointment, sterile dressing, and then out the door. Next patient please. We can't worry about tetanus, for we have no tetanus vaccine available.

Over the following days, it appears that the spirits of the refugees are gradually, yet persistently, being worn down. More people are getting on buses and going to the relocation centers, which some call internment camps. I doubt we will see riots of the magnitude we saw Sunday and Wednesday again, but who knows for sure?

16
Idomeni Eruption

Monday April 18, 2016
Idomeni
Lindsey Smith, FNP
(Lindsey Smith is a geriatric family nurse practitioner from Minnesota volunteering with Syrian American Medical Society.)

WE ARRIVE AT IDOMENI CAMP and park our makeshift medical van in our usual spot. I am ready for another day providing care for colds, coughs, headaches, tooth pain from lack of access to a dentist, and lice, which has spread throughout the camp. It's cold at night and without any wood the refugees are burning plastic to keep their families warm. The burning toxins in combination with residual effects from the tear gas attack the week before are causing a wide range of respiratory issues. We have seen many children with severe burns from these fires as their playground is also their tight living space. The hardest part for me to treat is the mental and emotional health as many people are presenting with anxiety induced insomnia and feelings of hopelessness. I have very little to give for this other than being present.

Mariah, an EMT from Utah, and I decide to take a walk. We wander past families going about their daily lives and people who have converted their tents into stores. They are selling fruits, bread, and other items while others are purchasing.

We walk past two men who have set up barber shop consisting of a chair sitting on the dirt and tarp material for a drape. They work tirelessly all day in the sun cutting hair for a camp of 12,000 people. Children line up to get ice cream from a truck and men stand in long lines to gather their family's food portions for the day. Today there is a strong police presence with riot gear and eager reporters lurking around every corner. The police remain calm but their presence makes me feel uneasy.

We return back to our position at the mobile health van and continue working with our medical team of volunteer health professionals. We work until mid-afternoon. Now it is time to pack up and head to town for lunch. Half of the team has already left.

Deborah is a lovely art teacher from New York who had been helping us with medications and supplies. She, Mariah and I decide to head further into the camp to check out a new school that was recently started by a group of people from Spain.

Suddenly, there is a fight nearby. I see a woman of about sixty years old fall to the ground amidst the crowd. We run over to help as people start yelling. Mariah and I begin assessing her. I can't get any information because of the language barrier since my Arabic is limited as is their English. The woman is having a seizure. She shakes violently and then afterward she has a facial droop, foaming around her mouth and her speech is slurred. Men come running with a stretcher to help us while the fighting continues around us.

Some are trying to help us get the poor woman on the stretcher, others are trying to help her to get up and walk, while others are pushing in to see what's happening.

Fighting continues. At one point I grab a baby lying on the ground and step away from the danger and chaos, leaving the elderly woman. The tension is escalating. A man is screaming and waving a metal stick. I don't know who he is after or what is really happening. Later, we find out that the elderly woman's pregnant daughter had been hit during the fight and the elderly woman was trying to protect her.

I don't know what to do. There is no way of controlling the spiraling situation. Finally, people disperse. Several refugees help us load the woman on the stretcher. We carry her to the nearest medical tent, which is being run by Doctors without Borders (Medecins sans Frontieres).

As we are moving the stretcher inside the tent, a crowd of forty or so people is running directly toward us. They are screaming in terror as they carry a man on a stretcher covered with blood. The woman on the stretcher is shoved aside.

A critically injured man is laid on the hard ground. He is unconscious and bleeding from his eyes, ears, nose, and mouth. It is obvious that we have only a few minutes to react, if there is any hope at all for his survival. The crowd is being whipped into a frenzy by all the horror. People are screaming. There is a lot of pushing. Medics and doctors begin advanced life support on this critical patient. Tensions are high and emotions are out of control.

I try to jump the small fence bordering the medic tent. It seems to be the safest way to get through the crowd. A young woman falls to the ground, passing out from emotional shock. Several people around me help. We douse her with cold water. She finally comes around. I use what little Arabic I know and get her to talk to me. "Focus and breathe," I tell her.

After a few minutes, I have to move on and get back to my elderly lady. She also desperately needs help. Dr Omar Al-Heeti, from our medical team, and MSF doctors are working feverishly on the critically injured man. His oxygen saturations are critically low, and he is losing blood rapidly. His oxygenation improves with their ventilatory support, but he remains comatose with a severe head crush injury.

I'm still with the young lady and I turn to the guy by me and tell him to stay with her. "Keep her cool and as calm as possible." He looks at me with desperate eyes and says, "but I'm only an electrician!" I reassure him as best I can and leave him on the rock-hard ground holding this poor, emotionally fatigued young woman.

Once again, I jump through the crowd and over the fence into what feels like a boxing ring where everybody is fighting for whatever they can do with the limited supplies we have and utter pandemonium reigns. I go back into the tent to find the elderly woman shaking, sweating and sobbing in distress.

Her husband sits by her holding her hand with pleading eyes. Her son stands at her feet rubbing water on them. He is attempting to comfort her and cool her down. I grab a translator and the son and husband open up. They tell me how she watched five of her children murdered in Syria and, ever since then, she has had these shaking episodes. They tell me how her pregnant daughter was hit in the fight. It set her off into an emotional breakdown, which seems to have triggered her seizure. They tell me she gets seizures about twice a month, but she never has been treated for epilepsy. I hold her hand, speak softly, and remain as calm as possible even though what I really want to do is throw myself on the floor and sob.

I feel helpless myself. What can I offer this woman and family? After all they have been through, they have no promise for what tomorrow holds, and now caught in the middle of this utter chaos and trauma all over again.

When will this end for these people? What can I possibly do? As I rub her back, I look out the window at the rest of my team working on the critically injured man. One doctor is holding his feet up. He has lost so much blood that his feet are blue. Later I find out that one of the medical providers is telling the others to keep giving care even if he dies. Because if they stop, he fears the crowd will become even more chaotic.

I know my elderly woman should go to the hospital, but now she refuses to go. The family tells me they heard that if you go to the hospital, they won't bring you back to the camp. They are afraid. They are hearing that many refugees at other camps are being deported back to Turkey. She wants to stay here with her family.

Meanwhile, more people are being brought in by stretchers. The critically wounded trauma patient's wife is brought in not responding and in emotional shock. His mother sits in the corner sobbing and rocking herself. I now hear the rest of the story. The critically injured man was fixing his family's tent when he tripped and fell onto the road and his head was run over by the rear wheel of a police bus, which weighs several tons and is the size of a standard school bus.

In a camp already saturated with tension and riot police, this is the fuel needed for a very volatile situation. Despite our calls for an emergency ambulance, it takes more than forty-five minutes for it to arrive. Doctors Without Borders is setting up areas in preparation for a disaster/mass casualty incident. We fear that if this man dies, things will escalate quickly.

I hear loud popping noises and look about one-hundred yards away to see police in riot gear moving through the crowd. We are trying our best to prepare for anything. The popping noises are sound bombs the police are letting off as warnings.

I can't process it all. I need a moment. I step into a portable toilet hoping for a moment alone so I can break down and let it all out without adding to the stress of the crowd. Once inside the close confines of this putrid smelly closed space, I realize this is not where I want to have my emotional breakdown. I have to hold it together for a while longer.

We survey the area on standby for a while. Things calm down gradually and we finally feel we can leave. Back at the medical van, I hand out suckers to kids and let them crawl all over me laughing and giggling trying to distract myself from what had just happened. After a while, we pack up and head back. Completely exhausted, we gather as a group at a restaurant in Polykastro to share meals and try to talk about anything but this tragedy we witnessed. We need some normalcy before we head right back into the fire of the evening clinic at Eko.

Normalcy is not a luxury these refugees can have, nor have any hopes for in the near future. I realize that the most traumatic day of my life was just another day for them. This place has become hell on earth. This is not the way humans should be forced to live, nor should other humans allow it.

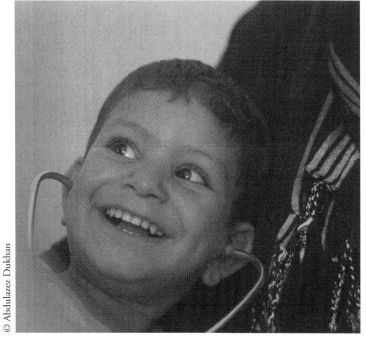

A rare smile during a checkup at the volunteer-operated clinics in the new military camps outside of Thessaloniki.

17
Women

Friday, April 22, 2016
Idomeni and Eko Camp
Kathy Stolarz DO
(Dr Stolarz is a family physician and women's health specialist from Maryland volunteering with SCM.)

Today is my seventh day in Greece, and my last day working at the camps. This thought alone is surreal. My reality has changed during my experience here. How can I even think about leaving? Per the usual routine, the group meets for breakfast. We have a small meeting, collect medications and supplies from our warehouse, and head to Idomeni Camp on the border.

We all know the routine by now and fall into our patterns. We open the back of the big white van, which acts as a pharmacy, and start to treat the refugees. They are just like us, from all walks of life. We treat artists, engineers, lawyers, and even other doctors.

Today is hot and there is no shade as far as the eye can see, but a line of refugees is building. So we hang a tarp on the side of the van to provide some shade. It's not much, but it helps. It's better than the conditions we had two days ago where the wind blew relentlessly. I can still feel the dirt in my eyes, ears, and nose, feel the grit of the dirt in my teeth and the burning in my lungs from inhaling all of the dust. I don't know how the refugees live in this, day in and day out.

One of the other volunteers brings me a man with a prescription that needs clarification. As one of the few volunteer physicians that conducts Women's Health, these cases are brought to me regularly. Via a translator, we clarify that his wife has had some kind of surgery at the hospital yesterday. He wants to know if she is still pregnant. They have a prescription for us to fill since the pharmacy at the hospital did not have the medication on hand. The prescription is for an antibiotic. She was able to get the pain medication. The story is not clear, so I ask someone who can speak Arabic to please accompany me to the tent where this woman is, so we can get more information and I can examine her.

Dr Omar Shamma, one of the best human beings I have ever met, accompanies me to the tent to help me translate since he himself does not practice Women's Health. Dr Omar is originally from Syria and is working in Saudi Arabia. He is volunteering with us here through Syrian American Medical Society (SAMS). I apologize that this takes him away from seeing other refugees in need, but we are short on translators and he is gracious. We walk for about five minutes before we reach one of the large UNHCR tents that is home to over a hundred refugees in bunks. We head to the back right corner, where under one of the bunks lays a woman on blankets on the ground, on her back and clearly in pain.

What happened yesterday? How far pregnant were you? What procedure did they do? She had been pregnant for an unknown amount of time, which is common as a refugee, since they are often too busy fleeing war to notice that they missed their period. Yesterday she started bleeding heavily and was taken to the hospital. They "cleaned out" her uterus or something to that effect to stop the bleeding. My heart was breaking for her. I knew the burden the refugees were placing on the medical system in Greece, but to not explain to the woman that she wasn't pregnant anymore? That's heartbreaking. And most likely, her lack of understanding was mainly due to a breakdown in communication because of the language and cultural barriers, lost in translation between Greek and Arabic.

In this moment I'm reminded of what a vulnerable state motherhood is, so much so, that it is specifically noted in Article twenty-five of the Universal Declaration of Human Rights. "Motherhood and Childhood are entitled to special care and assistance," it says. Where was this mother's special assistance now? Lying on the ground in a refugee camp unable to obtain the medications she needs, in pain, scared; not sure if she had lost her child or not.

With Dr Omar, we gently break the news that she has miscarried. You can tell by the looks on their faces that this has confirmed their fears. I encourage her to stay hydrated, take the pain medication, and assure her I will return with the antibiotics she needs.

Dr Omar and I return to the van. But now he is needed to see patients, so I return alone to provide her with the medication. Although we do not speak the same language, I'm able to express my condolences and she is able to express her gratitude. There is a connection between women during a loss like this that transcends language.

I start to head back to the van, but I don't make it farther than halfway through the tent before another mother grabs me. She points to her two-year-old daughter who is sleeping, and says, "Fever, fever." The child is drenched in sweat, and passed out cold. I am a little concerned and I need more information. So mom agrees we can go to the van for translation. I pick up the limp child, skin hot to the touch and dripping wet, and we start walking. About halfway to the van, the child wakes up and looks at me, a complete stranger carrying her. She does not scream, but immediately smiles. I wonder how starved for love and affection these refugee children must be.

We arrive at the van. With translation and exam, the diagnosis of an ear infection is fairly easy. The decision to give her amoxicillin is standard of care. Mixing up the medication is not so easy. All medication for children is weight-based. How do I weigh this child without a scale? Thanks to an average weight chart per age and gender from Dr Hena Ibrahim, our pediatrician, we can get close. Where do I find clean water to mix up the medication? Thankfully we have some bottled water for the volunteers to drink in the car; the alternative is for the family to wait for hours in the food line for their daily rationing of food and drinking water, which wouldn't even be enough. I'm able to give her enough for a day's doses, she will come back tomorrow for more.

After several hours in the sun, we start to wrap up. Dr Robina Mohammed Younis and I have to head out early to a Maternal-Fetal Health meeting at the Medecins sans Frontiers headquarters in Polykastro. She and I are the Women's Health providers of the group, both generalists who also provide prenatal and obstetric care back home. We will meet with the rest of the group for lunch.

Polykastro is the nearest city center to Idomeni Camp, so it's a home base for a lot of NGOs. It is also where our medication and supply warehouse is located. We find the MSF headquarters and join Ann Van Haver, the Belgian MSF midwife, who is running the meeting. She has asked all NGOs and individual providers who are providing maternal-fetal health in all of the surrounding camps to meet to coordinate our care.

Those present at the meeting include Medecins sans Frontiers, Salaam Cultural Museum, Syrian American Medical Society, Kitrinos (previously known as Off Track Health), Medics Bergen, Health Point Foundation, Nurture Project International (NPI), Bomberos en Accion, and independent midwives. We all share our current activities at the different campsites. It becomes clear that MSF is mainly coordinating the care at Idomeni Camp, and we (SCM/SAMS) are leading the coordination at Eko Camp. The midwives are caring for women at the smaller camps where there are no larger NGOs.

They are also doing "home visits" to tents at all the camps to reach women that may not venture out to other organizations for care. NPI is providing much needed breastfeeding aid for new mothers and infants.

It's not a perfect system, but I'm impressed that with everyone contributing, pregnant women in all of the campsites have at least some minimal access to care. Note that some of these camps are just a few tents next to a gas station, while Idomeni currently has around 12,000 people. The passion of this group is exhilarating. We review the protocols for getting women to the hospital for deliveries, Cesarean sections, and emergency procedures. We agree to try to create a registry of all pregnant women at our campsites, so that we can pass this information on when we leave and the next set of volunteers come.

Robina and I head back to meet with the others working with our SCM/SAMS mobile health team. After lunch, we all lie in the grass for a nap. We are all physically and emotionally drained, attempting to process all that has happened. We wonder how we will take this new information back to our old lives. How can we possibly communicate what we've seen to others? Can I accurately describe this level of human suffering and resilience all at once?

In the afternoon, we head to Eko Camp, which houses around 2200 refugees. Through the coordination of Kitrinos and another group of Swedish volunteers, we have obtained a large yellow van, which was driven across Europe and down through the Balkans from the Netherlands. It previously functioned as an ambulance and has an exam room in the back. Robina and I from SCM/SAMS had set this van up at the beginning of the week. It is to serve the women in the community and to serve as an emergency delivery room should a woman not be able to make it to the hospital in time. I cannot express what an incredibly huge contribution this is to women's health here. Refugee women in the camps live in tents with anywhere from five to over 250 people, depending on the size. Their only privacy is in the port-a-potties and showers. Prior to the van, there was no place for a woman to have a private exam.

Once we get the word out about the private space for women, we are treating urinary tract infections, vaginal infections, folliculitis, and providing prenatal care with much better precision. I have never felt like my medical skills were better put to use. Seeing the smile on a pregnant mother's face who is hearing her child's heart still beating in the womb, despite everything she has been through, especially fleeing the war, is absolutely priceless. There is no better feeling in the world than this and I could do it forever. When we all work together, amazing things can happen. It's through this that I touched a life, and really made a difference.

And while I have never felt more personally and professionally fulfilled, at the same time, I have never felt more helpless. Although I brought some joy to a woman today, I can't help her with her much bigger problems. I can't help her be granted asylum so that she can restart her life and raise her children. I can't help her reunite with family members she has left behind in a war-torn country. I can't bring back the family and friends she has lost. I feel fulfilled and helpless at the same time.

One of my patients comes by to check in and to say goodbye. She is seventeen years old and pregnant due to a forced marriage by her father, who beats her. Multiple organizations are working to try to help her, but resources are limited. She is just one of the many incredible women I have met, who smiles in the face of having been through so much already. We have reported her case to the relevant authorities at UNHCR, but it is not clear what if anything will be done about her plight. I will pass on her case on to the next set of Women's Health providers, but what can we really do other than give her medical care? How do we protect her from further physical harm? I'm feeling hopelessly helpless.

As I finish up my last shift in the Women's Health Van, or "Big Mamma" as we call it, I become more nostalgic. I'm going to miss my new friend Nour very much. She is a refugee who has been translating for me all week in the Women's Van. We have grown close. She is incredibly bright and kind. Nour, who is twenty years old, traveled from Syria with her twelve-year-old brother. Their parents could not afford the trip and are back in Syria, leaving Nour to raise him on her own as they progress through this uncertain journey. She was studying English literature back in Syria but her studies were cut short by the war. After working with me doing medicine, she lights up at the thought of becoming a doctor one day. She loves helping people, and she's good at it. But what chance does she have to accomplish this from a refugee camp? I pray that she is granted asylum somewhere, that someone else will see her brilliance and compassion. She and I are the same really. We both started as young girls with a passion for learning and helping others. I was just given the opportunity to do something with it. I give Nour a big hug goodbye, unsure of when or if I will ever see her again. I hope I will.

Postscript, September 2016:

Months later, Nour and I are in contact via social media. She has been moved to a government camp and there is no end in sight. She tells me how miserable she is: That she doesn't want to eat or leave the tent; that she no longer wants to translate for the volunteers; that she wants to die . . . that she would rather have died in Syria pursuing her dreams than wasting her life away in this camp. I encourage her to get out of the tent and try to stay busy, but all of the refugees I've kept in touch with are falling into deep depressions. After everything they've been through, they do not deserve this.

18
When? How?

April 29, 2016
Idomeni and Polykastro
Bill Dienst, MD

THE FORTY-YEAR-OLD MAN who stumbled in front of a Greek police bus while fixing his tent suffered a devastating crush injury to his head. He received immediate medical attention by Dr Omar Al-Heeti who works as part of our joint team of medical professionals from the Syrian American Medical Society (SAMS) and Salaam Cultural Museum (SCM), and with help from doctors from Medecins San Frontieres (MSF).

When the Greek ambulance arrived, Dr Omar traveled with the ambulance crew all the way to the rural Kilkis Hospital, providing positive pressure ventilation and suctioning the patient's airway. Transport time was over an hour. At Kilkis, this man received intubation from a Greek anesthesiologist. Due to massive facial injuries, the intubation was extremely difficult. He was then transferred to the medical center in Thessaloniki. He remained comatose and died from his injuries two days later. He leaves behind a grieving wife and four small children who are still stranded in a tent in the Idomeni camp.

On April 26, 2016, the Greek Ministry of Interior and Administrative Reconstruction issued the following notice in Arabic, Kurdish, Urdu and Farsi to refugees living in the camps around Idomeni:

Information to Refugees—Migrants

You are in Greece and you are guests in this country. It is your obligation to follow the rules and instructions of the Greek State.

The borders, and this is not a responsibility of the Greek government, are and will remain closed. This settlement does not cover any of your basic everyday needs. It will end its operations. You should move to the camps run by the Greek State, in a fast and coordinated way, under the responsibility of the Greek authorities.

The Greek State gives you the opportunity to stay in the temporary receptions facilities (camps, hotels, settlements and other facilities) in various areas in the country.

These facilities are open but are guarded and controlled so that you and your families are safe. There you will find food, medical care, clothes and personal hygiene items.

While in these reception facilities, you can move freely, going out and coming in, but you must return back at a specified time and you must observe the Operation Regulations. If you do not observe these rules, you will lose your right to stay there.

You must also register. Soon after you enter the reception facility, the Greek Authorities will give you information on your right to apply for asylum in Greece, and the option of relocation in another EU member state for those fulfilling the terms and conditions of the relocation programme. You will also receive information on the family reunification procedure so as to reunite with members of your family in EU member states.

You will also receive legal and financial aid so as to return to your country of origin in case your asylum application is rejected or in case you wish to return. You are requested to follow the orders and instructions of the competent members of staff who will tell you how to leave this settlement in an orderly manner and how to be transported safely to the reception facilities.

Many of the refugees, and some of the international volunteers who have put so much time and effort into developing the healthcare and humanitarian infrastructure at Idomeni camp, found this notice very upsetting. Some are angry with the Greek government for suggesting that Idomeni camp will soon be dismantled. MSF, Medecins du Monde, Praxis, ICRC, Save the Children and hundreds of smaller NGO's like us have invested tens of thousands of dollars trying to make life tolerable here. Infrastructure is still being developed such as new showers, toilets, makeshift schools, etc.

Now we are finally catching up with the health care and humanitarian demands of this trapped population. For the first time, a dental clinic started operations five days ago, fulfilling overwhelming dental needs. We hope to have similar dental services at the other gas station camps soon.

Those of us who have been here awhile arrived to witness long queues of people shivering in the cold mud and torrential downpours of late winter rains. We had limited supplies and had to tell many people waiting in long lines, "No, we don't have the resources to help you right now with your problem." Many of these limitations have been slowly but surely getting better.

The cold winter rains have subsided. Now, in spite of a few days of tear gas, sound grenades, rubber bullets and high winds, which rip some of the tents to shreds, the overall weather and living conditions, are improving. It is no longer too cold, but soon, it will be too hot. I shudder to think what will happen when the Holy Month of Ramadan starts in June and people are fasting from sunrise to sunset during the longest days of the year and summer swelter. We may then be seeing heat stroke, dehydration, kidney stones etc. The treatment for heat stroke is to cool the patient down. But we have no air-conditioned shelters, no ice, only tents, which can get hotter on the inside than on the outside during the daytime under these conditions. The nearest hospital in the town of Kilkis is over an hour away, and ambulances are limited.

No, the situations at Idomeni, Eko, BP, and Hara gas stations are not tenable in the long run. We cannot blame the Greeks either, for they did not ask at all for this refugee crisis. It was put upon them. The farmers in the tiny village of Idomeni (population 154) want their farmland back, and their way of life; and who can blame them? The railway station needs to reopen again soon.

This stalemate has to end sooner or later; maybe sooner would even be better than later, especially with the hot summer sun approaching. The problem that those of us serving the refugees face now has to do with timing. There seems to be no way for us to accurately predict when the camps here will be dismantled. Meanwhile, we continue to develop further infrastructure to meet fundamental human needs for those who can't wait.

© Abdulazez Dukhan

A man sits by a camp fire into the night in Eko Camp, an unofficial camp located down the highway from the border crossing between Greece and Macedonia.

19
Escape

May 2016
Polykastro
Bill Dienst, MD

IT IS MID-AFTERNOON IN THIS SMALL TOWN in the Macedonian region of northern Greece. We have just finished our mobile health clinic at Idomeni camp. We are resting before gearing up for the evening clinic at Eko gas station camp. Dr Anas Nader is a Syrian-Canadian who practices emergency medicine in London. He and I sit while taking our afternoon lunch. We sit and we talk. The question is a simple one: What needs to be done to end the civil war in Syria and the endless wars in the Middle East? The answers are much more complicated. They have grown increasingly more complex following more and more military interventions over the last several decades.

These wars have created this massive crisis of human suffering that we see right in front of us and what we can see is only a small portion of the Greater Crisis . . . the worst refugee crisis since the end of World War II. This crisis is guaranteed to haunt Europe, the Middle East and North Africa for years and perhaps generations to come. The people whom we care for did not choose this mess, or leave their homelands by preference. They chose what they thought would be their least bad option . . . in many cases, fleeing for their lives. And now they find themselves stranded indefinitely in this hellhole.

How do we escape from this mess? How do we put all these fragmented pieces of humanity back together again and make things whole? The answers are as clear as mud. But we can learn from comparable horrific conflicts throughout the world, which have somehow been put to rest: South Africa under Apartheid, El Salvador and Rwanda. Even Lebanon, Syria's neighbor to the west was considered a hopeless "failed state" back in the 1980s. However, after fifteen years of Civil War, Lebanon has put itself back together again, more or less. Now, Lebanon is overrun with refugees fleeing from Syria. None of these countries are perfect societies, but they are much better now than they were when civil wars were raging. There is still hope for Syria too; even

Iraq, Afghanistan, and Palestine. But for this to happen, world leaders need to start thinking more creatively and get out of their boxes.

First we must ask, "How did this all start?" We must go back and summarize. It's arbitrary, but World War I and the decline of the Ottoman Empire is a good place to start. The British and French foreign ministers, Sykes and Picot, drew the borders of the modern Middle East in 1916. They tried to impose nation-states in a region that was collectively ruled by the Ottomans, and had no borders. Unfortunately, the borders that Sykes and Picot created were based more on French and British imperial designs, not on the natural order of different ethnicities who lived in the region.

For example, the area where the Kurds live was split among four nations: Iraq, Turkey, Syria and Iran. Kuwait, which was already known then to have a lot of oil, was carved out of what became Iraq, leaving Iraq with minimal access to the sea through the Persian Gulf. Lebanon was carved from Syria, intended to become a Christian enclave aligned with Christian Imperial Europe. There were a mixture of different ethnicities Lebanon too, and things didn't turn out the way that the European imperial powers had planned. And then there was the Balfour declaration in 1917, advocating a Jewish homeland in Palestine. Never mind the concerns of Palestinian Arabs who already lived there.

Proxy Wars

Monarchs designed to become quislings of the West were put in power in these client states. Later on, some of these monarchs were overthrown, while others still remain, as in Saudi Arabia. Let's now fast-forward to the end of World War II, the Holocaust, and the founding of the Jewish State of Israel. This founding resulted in the systematic displacement of three-quarters of a million Palestinian refugees to the West Bank, Gaza, Jordan, Lebanon, Syria, and beyond, where they and their descendants languish today.

In 1949, Shukri Al-Quwatli, the democratically elected leader of Syria, was overthrown in a CIA-inspired coup, under the leadership of Allen Dulles at the CIA. An unstable period of coups and counter-coups followed, and Al-Quwatli was restored to power again in 1955 through popular elections.

In 1953, Mohammed Mosaddegh, the democratically elected President of Iran was overthrown by the CIA when he tried to nationalize his country's oil reserves. Shah Reza Pahlavi, with dictatorial powers, was put in his place to act as a quisling for the West. This went well for Western oil interests until the Islamic revolution in 1979.

In 1957, the CIA again attempted to overthrow President Shukri Al-Qu-watli of Syria. This attempt was unsuccessful, and resulted in the unintended consequence of pushing the Syrian government into the hands of the Soviets (and after the fall of the Soviet Union, the Russians). In the US, the 1957 Bruce-Lovett Report uncovered CIA coup plots in Jordan, Syria, Iran, Iraq, and Egypt. In Iraq, one of these CIA-funded coup attempts was subsequently successful, resulting in the Ba'ath Party coming to power. Among their ranks was their future leader, Saddam Hussein.

Both Iraq and Syria were each lead by political parties called Ba'ath. Both Ba'ath parties shared some similarities in that they were nationalist and secular. In each however, there were privileged ethnicities within the greater population. In Syria prior to the Al-Assad regime, the Sunni Muslim majority had been the privileged population and the Alawite minority was disadvantaged. This situation became reversed after Hafez Al-Assad came to power. Due to blowback from the CIA coup attempts described above, the Syrian government, Hafez Al-Assad, and later his son Bashar, became even more deeply involved as formal clients of the Soviet Union and later on the Russians. Subsequently, they also aligned themselves with Shi'ite entities, including Iran and Lebanon's Hezbollah, a Shi'ite militia, founded in 1983. Hezbollah had been instrumental in forcing the Israelis back from an 18-year occupation of southern Lebanon. Iran and China have also lined up on this side of the proxy conflict in Syria.

Saddam Hussein's Iraq was also a Ba'ath party, but that regime favored minority Sunni over majority Shia. This was opposite of the situation in Syria. Iraq had been an opportunistic ally of the Americans in the 1980s when, after the Islamic Republic coup, it launched a war against Iran. This war was actively encouraged and Iraq was actively supported by the US. There is an old adage, which says, "The enemy of our enemy is our friend." Saddam Hussein used chemical warfare agents brought from Germany, the US, and France against the Iranians and the Kurds, while the Americans continued to support him before, during, and afterward.

But when Saddam invaded Kuwait in 1991 and threatened Western oil interests, the tables were turned. All of a sudden, Saddam's Iraq became the enemy. The US government later claimed that chemical warfare was outside the limits of the Geneva Convention, and used this as one of many pretexts for attacking Iraq in 1991. Successive hardships followed: First there was Gulf War I followed by no-fly zones during the 1990's, and then Gulf War II. In 2003, Saddam was compared to Hitler in the Western media. The Bush administration and mainstream media pundits claimed that he had weapons of mass destruction, a claim that later on, proved to be false. A full scale American ground invasion and military occupation followed. Saddam Hussein and his Ba'athist regime were overthrown.

Iraq went from being a secular country, which was the most technologically advanced in the Arab world, to a sectarian fragmented failed state, heavily manipulated by American and other Western interests. During the years that followed, the tables have been turned again. Shi'a elements have most of the power, and ironically, they align themselves with Iran. Iraq has fragmented into different areas controlled by different factions, many that resemble theocracies. Among the refugees we see today at Idomeni, the largest numbers are Syrian. The second largest numbers are from Iraq. The third and fourth largest groups are from Afghanistan and Pakistan. They are refugees from another endless proxy war that began in the 1980s when the US supported the *Mujahidin* who opposed the Soviet invasion. These Holy Warriors have since evolved into the *Taliban* and *Al-Qa'ida*.

During Saddam Hussein's reign in Iraq, one had to be a Ba'ath party member to have any status or professional role in society. But after the American invasion in 2003, Ba'ath party members were outcasts and deliberately excluded from any future role. After revelations about widespread torture following the Abu Ghraib prison scandal, more and more disenfranchised military members of the former Ba'ath Party began joining the Iraqi resistance against the American occupation. Groups like *Al-Qa'ida in Iraq* developed where *Al Qa'ida* had never existed before.

Later on, *Al-Qa'ida in Iraq* faded in its influence after its leader, Abu Musab Al-Zarqawi was killed by a US airstrike in 2006. In about 2012, another splinter organization, which became DA'ISH (ISIS), formed and became prominent. In February 2014, Al Qa'ida formally severed its relationship with ISIS over issues having to do with ISIS's sectarianism against Shi'a Muslims and other issues[4]. ISIS grew and spilled over into Syria. It is being funded by proxy Sunni Salafist sources in Saudi Arabia, the United Arab Emirates, Qatar and Turkey. Many of its commanders are former military men from Saddam Hussein's Ba'ath party. While under captivity by ISIS, Vincent (not his real name, described previously in Chapter 14, "Vincent's story"), also met ISIS soldiers while he was being tortured who had been *Mujahedeen* in Afghanistan supported by Americans while fighting the Soviets back in the 1980s. Through these endless wars, we have created many lifetime professional mercenaries with no other skill set. So there is something to be said to the argument that Western military actions have, directly or indirectly, created the current entity known as ISIS today.

And at the United Nations, which should be the world government body for conflict resolution, these proxy wars are exacerbated. Despite a widespread consensus in the UN General Assembly for action to curtail human rights violations by both the Israeli Government and the Al-Assad regime, resolutions never make it past the Security Council. Resolutions critical of Israel are routinely vetoed by the United States, while resolutions that are critical of the Al-Assad regime in Syria are routinely vetoed by Russia and China. So the powers that be, which are the very powers that could do substantial things to solve these problems, are a major part of the problems themselves. Their leaders are too caught up in geopolitical *Real-politik* to be able to show any genuine concern for human suffering.

The Americans and some of their Western allies were never opposed by any major superpower in Iraq or Libya. Consequently, they were able to force regime change in these countries. And now these two countries are failed states, where ISIS has gained substantial influence. The situation in Syria is similar in terms of the humanitarian disaster, but it is also different because of the Russian alliance with the Al-Assad regime. We cannot force regime change here. So now Syria is condemned to this current horrific stalemate of a perpetual proxy war far removed from the needs of the Syrian people and in which no one side can win.

Divided and Conquered

The Syrian experiment with the Arab Spring was crushed violently by the Al-Assad regime and further exacerbated by military support of the opposition. Western elements covertly supported a military response called, "The Free Syrian Army." Many of these Free Syrian Army forces later aligned themselves with Al-Nusra Front, which is loosely affiliated with Al-Qa'ida. These elements crumbled further and American weaponry made its way into the hands of ISIS, both in Iraq and in Syria. ISIS has been supported by elements from our so-called allies in the Gulf States and from Turkey.

So now things in Syria are extremely polarized due to this climate of perpetual proxy war. If you are still living in Syria and want to be protected, you either need to be affiliated with the Al-Assad regime, which favors Alawite, Christian and other minorities, or with ISIS, which supports extremist Salafist Wahhabi elements who are a minority within the greater Sunni population. The Syrian, Iraqi, Kurdish and Yazidi refugees we see in Eko and Idomeni camp are largely those who just want a stable life and refuse to take sides. They don't want to send their sons to fight and die in sectarian wars, or geo-political wars based on oil, or who controls proposed oil pipelines through Syria being stoked by proxies of Russia, the USA, the Iranians, or the Gulf States.[5] These people are those caught in the middle. Their current stalemate of being stranded in northern Greece is their least bad option. But as the stalemate and uncertainty continue, more and more are telling us they want to go back to Syria and meet their fate, even if it means death.

Reconciliation towards Ending the Refugee Stalemate

So how do we finally put an end to all this mess? The short answer is: Stop pouring more gasoline on the fire!!!

As those in the substance abuse/chemical dependency recovery business like to ask, "How's it working for ya?" World politicians need to enroll in 12-step programs for war addiction. Insanity is doing the same thing over and over again and expecting different results. Every time there is a bomb blast in Paris or Brussels, Western politicians act astonished, as if their previous actions in the Middle East, which have led to widespread death, destruction, chaos, heartbreak, alienation and disillusionment, have had nothing to do with the attacks. Right wing politicians react with Islamophobia in the West, which compounds the unfolding disasters even further. When there is a similar ISIS attack of equal or greater proportions in Beirut, Istanbul or Baghdad, Western leaders and pundits remain indifferent to these widespread episodes of human suffering, which are happening with much greater degrees of magnitude in the Middle East, as if only Western lives matter.

Politicians take more knee-jerk reactions like the previously mentioned ill-fated regime changes in Iraq and Libya, and by bombing more ISIS targets in Iraq, Syria, Yemen, Somalia, and other locations. These attacks hit some intended targets, but also many more civilians are caught in the wrong place at the wrong time. Then a bomb goes off on some airplane . . . a Russian airliner climbing out of Sharm El Sheikh, Egypt or another airliner, returning to Egypt from Paris. More civilians in Iraq and Syria get killed and maimed "in retaliation." And few in the West or in Russia even care.

The survivors of these Middle Eastern martyrs demand more and more revenge for Western and Russian attacks. This polarizes the situation further. More Western and Russian targets are hit. Here we go again, whirling around and around; Deja Vu all over again.

Attempts to overthrow the Al-Assad regime through military means are extremely dangerous and futile while it is being directly supported by Russia. A direct military confrontation between the US and Russia risks a dangerous escalation with minimal benefit to either party. Indirect covert military support of Syrian rebel groups has clearly been counter-productive, with a large proportion of our weapons inadvertently winding up in the wrong hands like ISIS. Taking on the Russian Air Force while trying to impose a no-fly-zone, as Hillary Clinton has suggested, is sheer insanity. It could bring on World War III.

Have we had enough yet? When does it stop? What about this massive humanitarian catastrophe we are creating? Should we all react like Donald Trump, put our heads in the sand and just try to build more walls and drop more bombs? Or should we show more compassion? Is this what Western Democracy is supposed to be about? Or is there a different way?

There has to be a different way. We need a UN sponsored moratorium on weapons to the Middle East. More weapons are not making anybody safer; quite the opposite. Our leaders, like Secretary of State John Kerry have said as much: That there are no military solutions to the problems in Syria; the same goes for countries like Yemen, Iraq, Libya, Afghanistan and Palestine/Israel.

Dropping bombs on ISIS targets or covert military actions against the Syrian regime are having counter-productive polarizing effects. Invading Syria with ground troops and imposing another military occupation is unlikely to improve matters, especially when American credibility in the region is at an all-time low. Ground troops and military occupations have not improved matters in Afghanistan or Iraq. They are unlikely to improve matters in Israel/Palestine or in Syria either. The only people benefiting are the weapons manufacturers, the merchants of death.

We need truth and reconciliation commissions in the various countries involved. These were very helpful in resolving conflicts at the end of Apartheid in South Africa and at the end of the genocide in Rwanda and the civil war in El Salvador.

As a superpower, the United States needs to end American and Israeli exceptionalism and get back to standing up for what we say we are about: Liberty and Justice for All, Freedom of Religion for All and Separation of Religion and State. No more factionalism and sectarianism. No more dividing and conquering, playing one side off against the other. And we should not be supporting the concept of a Jewish State any more than we should be supporting an Islamic Republic or a Christian Nation.

We need to partner with other nations, including the Russians, the Chinese, the Iranians, and our partners in Europe and in the Middle East. We need to encourage the active participation of both government and civil society organizations within the war-afflicted nations of the Middle East themselves. We must emphasize diplomatic interventions and de-emphasize military ones. Refusing to negotiate only perpetuates more endless wars, which are easy to spark into huge infernos, but extremely difficult to put out. Only when the warring factions in the region are no longer being backed into corners can things cool down as they did in Lebanon. Extremist positions will gradually be abandoned. Most of the people in the region do not want to live this way.

In Palestine/Israel, there are only four possible futures: 1) The End of the World (which I am categorically against). 2) Keeping the situation as it is now, with endless Apartheid and endless war. 3) The Two State solution, with Israel limited to its pre-1967 borders and Palestine in the West Bank, Gaza and East Jerusalem, or 4) The one state solution: A democratic, secular government in Israel/Palestine with equal rights for all.

The one state solution is now the most long term viable answer for Israel and Palestine. Continuous settlement expansion of the West Bank and the longstanding imprisonment of the 1.8 million people in Gaza have made the two-state solution, which might have been possible twenty years ago, no longer viable.

As things cool down across the region, and societies have a chance to heal and rebuild, other possibilities may gradually emerge. Economic cooperation similar to what happened in Europe after World War II through entities like the European Union, can also happen in the Middle East. In the meantime, the wealthier Middle Eastern nations, Europeans, North Americans and Russians need to find creative ways to cooperate toward findings homes for the vast exodus of refugees that our policies have created and exacerbated. Put all the money that we have squandered and continue to squander in weapons toward reconstruction and rebuilding. As the saying goes, "We broke it, now we need to fix it."

Pony of Mine

20
Syrian Sonnets

May, 2016
Eko Refugee Camp
Ahmed Younso
(Ahmed Younso is a university educated Syrian refugee and poet who has been living in a tent for months at Eko.)

Racist God
God called Sam, so Pallid and White
Almost makes you Blind
So Sensitive Crying for Pageant Queens and Seals
In some Far Off Land

Love Puppies so much
Feed them Hug them Treat them Better
Than this Child

Once he wanted to Paint his Room
He killed Billions of Babies
To make the Color Bright

They are not like Him
Nor Neither their Name

He took their Eyeballs to make Cool Light
His Airplanes destroyed every Flower and Innocent Voice
To make him Sing Loud

"Every Man, Woman, Child, Flower, Stone not like Me
Deserves to Die," he Replied.

Eko Station

If you are in Eko Station
You will see real Dehumanization

You don't have the Right
To Love, to Hate
Or even to Get Inspiration

You are just a Small Number:
Unfortunate Collateral Damage to the Whims of
Other Greedy Nations

They will never ever see you as Another Human Being
Just a Creature threatened by Deportation

Sometimes I Wish That
I was Dead in Syria
Better than Being Stranded in this Fucking Situation

But we will Never Break Down
We of Strong Composition
To Cross the Deserts, the Mountains, the Borders and the Sea
To your Last Destination
To be Syrian means to Suffer in All the Different Ways you can Imagine

Red Indians

We are the new Red Indians
Similar to Cats and Dogs
Maybe below

When I hear the Big Fat Liars
Talking about Human Rights
I want to Explode

Please Mister Civilized World
Find Some Tobacco or Shoes to Chow

You don't see the Tears
Or the Massacres in My Homeland
Or You don't have a Clue

Those People dying Everyday
Just Humans like You
The Human without Humanity
Like an Animal and Maybe worse
That's so True

A Bird

A Bird saw a small Window
And it wanted to rest on a Hot Day
The Bird saw lots of People in that Room
Almost Dead with no Hope

Anyway, he asked, Why are you here in this Jail like a Slave?
One said,
I am in a Land where you get Punched because you are a Human and sent
to a Grave
Can you do Something for Me?
Tell my Mother that when they executed me I was so Brave

Tell my Lover, I love her and when I think of Her
I feel Free and Safe
Tell my friends, I miss them
And I miss our Games and Jokes
And that day when we Broke the Door

Tell the Roses in my Yard
I can't Forget their Scent or Colors
And they helped me with Girls
To lure Poor Humans

The bird said, You made me Cry
You even dried my Tear
Your Pain is so Deep
Like the Oceans

It's an Arrow in my Heart or a Spear
I will tell them your Words
and all the Things you Said
My dear, the bird said
I am so lucky that I am

The Last Night

Missile and Death talking in the sky of Syria:
In one of those Nights of War
The Missile told the Death
Why should we Wake those Kids from their Sleep?
Can't we ignore?

Death said that's not our fault
It's Fate and we can't ignore Fate
That's for sure

The missile cried and said
I didn't decide to do this
To kill, to Destroy, and More

Don't be Sad my Friend
I will let them sleep, but forever
I will take them to the heavens of Eden
Because they are so Pure

Their innocent Souls will be the Crown upon my Head
And the Endless Lighthouse for the Sore to open your Eyes
To feel their pain
It's your Soul's Cure

21
"Prepare a Burial"

Night 47 . . . 3:00 am, Sometime in late May, 2016
Eko Refugee Camp
Mohammad J Deen
(Mohammad J Deen is a Palestinian-American registered nurse from Chicago volunteering with Kitrinos.)

I DO A WALK-THROUGH OF THE CAMP to make sure everyone is OK. I check up on the patients who visited the clinic earlier and make sure to check up on our chronic patients in the camp as well. Typically, I don't do this at 3:00 am. I usually do this at midnight, because I try to catch a few hours of sleep before frantic parents worried about their child's fever wake me up.

3:30 am: Another walk-though. I find myself doing this walk through every thirty minutes on Night 47. Why?

Well . . .

Twenty hours earlier, a six-year-old Syrian refugee boy named Alyamman with a very rare neuromuscular disorder was given hours-to-days to live by very respected senior doctors who work with us. He and his family are residents here in Eko Refugee Camp and live in a tent across from our mobile clinics. His father Wasel was told, "We need to prepare a burial because your son is not going to make it."

Wasel has been going to an organization that is supposed to be handling the problems of refugees with special needs, like medical conditions that are too complicated to manage out of our local mobile health vans, or our local primary care camp clinic operated by Medecins sans Frontieres. These patients are supposed to be referred to specialists working at Greek hospitals in the city of Thessaloniki or sometimes Athens. But these kinds of refugee referrals frequently fall through the cracks. In the cases of Alyamman's and that of many others there has been extremely poor followed through. This child has never been sent to a hospital or to a safer living environment as has been promised by different NGOs working with Greek health care authorities.

The Greek health care system has been underfinanced and overwhelmed, even before this refugee crisis, especially in rural areas similar to this one here at Eko Camp and the nearby small town of Polykastro. Often when we do successfully refer to the urban centers, they typically treat the initial acute problems of fever, cough, etc. without investigating further; like further investigating the underlying chronic illness. In Alyamman's case, this is now ultimately leading to his decline and imminent demise.

"We need to prepare a burial" is probably the one thing a father never wants to hear. I refuse to accept this statement either, even by these very well-respected doctors. Why? Maybe it's my stubbornness in seeing a desperate father about to lose his child, or maybe just the mere fact that this father left war-torn Syria to go to Turkey, and hence into the dark wave-tossed night across the Aegean Sea on a rubber boat. He and his family have been living in a tent for three months . . . all in a search for better treatment for his son and his family. I cannot allow myself to simply watch a boy die in the refugee camp without trying harder to save him.

Earlier that day, I was told by other health care providers to just let him go. "Why are you going to prolong his suffering?" they asked. Maybe I was not trying to prolong his suffering; maybe I wanted to help him see what it's like not to suffer. After all, he is just six years old. He has lived five of his young years in conflict and war.

"What are you going to do, Mohammad?" said one senior doctor earlier that day. I said I would do whatever it takes to help keep him alive, although at that point, I may have been in denial. I didn't care that these senior physicians, who have been practicing medicine longer than I have been alive, were ready to give up on the boy. By that point, I had already placed every single piece of medical equipment that I had inside the tent of this dying boy.

Night 47, 4:00 am: I can't sleep. Alyamman is breathing three times a minute and his oxygen saturations are very low. I'm not sure if I need to put a tube down his throat, or just see if he can stick it out and bounce back. Sure enough, as the morning comes, his oxygen status improves, but his condition overall is getting worse. His poor nutrition, medical history, and poor living conditions for months make this fight so much harder. At this point, he really does have only hours-to-days to live if he does not urgently receive adequate specialty healthcare.

Night 47, 4:10 am: I make a very important phone call to a doctor from Switzerland who had seen Alyamman a few days prior in Eko camp. Dr Matthias Keller has had previous success in moving vulnerable patients to proper care facilities in Switzerland. My hope is that his evaluation will get this child out and get him the care he needs. This doctor is our last hope. We have to get this boy out of the refugee camp. Dr Matthias tells me I need to wait until 1:00 pm for an answer. I can't wait because we're not sure if the boy can survive that long. But we have no other options.

The coming hours are full of confusion and blame amongst our team after a well-meaning but ill-timed Facebook post goes viral, contributing to the logistical chaos. CNN catches wind of it and runs the story. Now every NGO wants to take Alyamman to a hospital in Greece. Sounds good, right? No! Because, I have higher hopes for this boy and his family. The other parties are three months too late. A team of volunteers and I are trying to get him and his family out of Greece to Switzerland, because it's his only hope for long term survival and a better future. We are no longer looking for another band aid; we want definitive chronic care tailor-made to this boy and his rare condition.

1:00 pm finally comes around. I get a call from Dr Matthias. "We are 90% there! But I need to call you back at 5:00 pm." We need to wait a few more hours for confirmation from the Swiss government. I wait anxiously by my phone for several hours more when I finally get the call.

"We've got the ok! Get him to the Swiss embassy in Athens as soon as possible and let's fly him out tomorrow!" I go to the family to inform them of this good fortune. I walk into their tent, stand silent for a few seconds and smile. I look Wasel in the eyes and finally say, "Pack your bags, it's time to go!" Immediately, there is a roar in the tent followed by tears of joy.

I'm shocked and full of mixed emotions, which are somewhere between happiness and melancholy. Happy that Alyamman is going to be leaving this refugee camp, yet sad and somewhat frustrated because it has taken such a dramatic decline in his health, a miracle from Switzerland, a combination of my stubbornness and the father's stubbornness for us to get to a solution. We didn't give up on this boy, and as a result, we're taking him to his new home!

6:00 pm: We are packing and getting ready to go. This is not going to be an easy task for me. I was already up all the previous night making sure this kid stayed alive long enough to get him out. Now, I find myself needing to drive seven hours south to Athens so we can fly out the next day. At this point, I don't care that I haven't showered in days. I don't care that I haven't slept in days. I'm on an emotional high, a high I have never felt before! I'm going to get this kid down to Athens no matter what. But I can't do it alone. I need to take someone with me. The best person who can tag along is Petros Tsetris, a Greek national who has been volunteering with us in the camp. He can help bridge all the inevitable language gaps between the Greek authorities and us. After all, we're driving in the middle of the night, seven hours through rural Greece to reach Athens.

6:15 pm: The heartfelt goodbyes are poignant. Many refugees living in the camp find themselves saying their farewells to this family while I prepare myself mentally for the next challenge: getting this boy to another country. The goodbyes . . . beautiful scenes full of happiness, sadness, and hope, all blended into one between the refugees, who will remain stranded at Eko, and the departing family, who are moving on to their ultimate destination in Switzerland.

1 am: Nearly 48 hours after we were told that this boy wasn't going to survive and that we should plan the burial, we find ourselves in the house of a total stranger getting passport photos before our Swiss embassy appointment later this morning. We need them prior to arriving at the embassy. After this slight detour, we have passport photos in one hand, paper work in the other, and we're back on the road to Athens. We are seeing all smiles from this family of five: a husband, a wife, two beautiful daughters and one very ill little boy.

3:00 am: We finally arrive in Athens, tired, excited, and anxiously anticipating the next step.

8:00 am: We arrive at the Swiss embassy and receive the visas.

6:00 pm: We board the plane: just like that, we're on the plane! This is a miracle! But the hard part is just getting started. Prior to take off, I am questioned by the pilot. "How come no one told me about this sick boy?" I try my best to assure him that he will be stable to fly. I explain that critical care transport is what I do for a living, and this is just another day in the office for me (Well . . . not! I have no team with me, I barely have the essential medical equipment needed to keep him alive, and we all will be 30,000 feet in the air on a commercial flight.) But what other choice do we have? Either this boy dies a slow painful death in Greece, or he succumbs on the plane, or he makes it. The pilot decides to trust me. The plane takes off. The higher the plane ascends, the lower Alayamman's oxygen saturation dips:

0 feet: Oxygen saturation 93%

12,000 feet: Oxygen saturation 85%

30,000 feet: Oxygen saturation between 58% to 62%.

Any saturation below 60% would be serious even in the best medical environments. He needs oxygen. His lungs can't take the decrease in atmospheric pressure. I request my first tank of oxygen.

"How long does this last?" I ask. "You have high and low options. You get fifteen minutes on the high," the stewardess replies. "How many tanks do you have?"

"We have four tanks total."

I do the math. If I use the high flow end, I have only one hour of oxygen and then two additional hours remaining on the flight.

Three tanks of oxygen later, playing between the high and low settings for the duration of the flight, we finally land in Switzerland! His oxygen saturations manage to stay in the high 90's on the plane with the help of the oxygen tanks, so I know he is still fighting. He's fighting to stay alive, fighting for his family, fighting for his own better future.

We are off the plane and heading towards the exit. An ambulance is waiting for us at the exit door. I will never forget exiting the plane and walking the final fifty feet carrying the boy and then the feeling of immense relief when we finally reach the ambulance. He starts smiling at me, as if he knows that his family has made it to a better place. My eyes well up with tears.

Night 49: This child is now in a state-of-the-art pediatric hospital. I am still wide awake. I can't believe that forty-eight hours prior to all of this, I was swatting bugs off of this tiny boy's face trying to listen to breath sounds, feeling hopeless in a tent in the middle of a highway petrol station refugee camp thousands of miles away from home.

Postscript: Since Night 47, this boy has come a long way. He has been discharged from the hospital and now he is at home with his family in Basel, Switzerland. Not only is he getting proper treatment, he is also the only reason that his family made it out of the refugee camp. This boy was the reason they left Syria, and now he is the reason they made it to Switzerland and to a better life.

Alyamman was lucky. The sad thing is that when I return to the Eko refugee camp back in Greece a few days later, I find at least ten similar stories like his, other children who are struggling to survive another day. They're very sick, but they're not dying, not yet.

We never prepared a burial for this boy, but I am afraid we may have just taken a rain check for the next child who faces death. Because this took a miracle, and in these refugee camps, miracles don't come around too often

1 inch = 200 miles approx.

III
Military Camps

22
What I Have Learned

May 27, 2016,
Back home in Omak, Washington, USA
Bill Dienst, MD

WHEN THE MASS MIGRATION TO EUROPE via Greece and other destinations pinnacled a year or so ago, the world was caught off guard. Politicians in the USA and Europe, along with their client tyrants and renegades in the region, had felt free to prosecute their endless wars in the Middle East. They showed minimal concern for the disastrous humanitarian consequences and the repercussions that would occur.

Part One of this story began in Lesvos and many other Greek Islands near Turkey. Boats started coming ashore in huge numbers. Other boats capsized at sea and bodies washed ashore. Greek farmers and fishermen responded as best they could, but the task was overwhelming. The world's conscience slowly awoke and governmental, non-governmental organizations and other civil society groups built rescue infrastructure in efforts to mitigate the human suffering, which resulted from this humanitarian catastrophe. Through the fall and winter of 2015-2016 these efforts continued. By winter, creatively elaborate and multi-dimensional infrastructures had been put in place on Greek Islands to care for refugees who had been coming ashore in huge numbers.

But by March 2016, on islands like Lesvos, we rescuers discovered that we were all dressed up, with nothing much to do. The European Union reached agreement with Turkey to employ the Turkish Coast Guard, Frontex ships, and NATO ships to block smugglers from taking refugees across the straights.

For the refugees, the trip across the Aegean Sea to the Greek Islands had previously been the most difficult part of the voyage. The next steps were to be relatively easy: become registered, take a ferry to the Greek Mainland, and then follow the Balkan trail to Germany or to other destinations in northern Europe, where they would join with other friends and family members who had gone before them to start a new life.

But by February/March 2016, Part Two of this story emerged. Germany had already absorbed about a million refugees by this time. All of a sudden, the rules changed. Hungary and Bulgaria had already blocked their borders. This was followed by Austria, and then Slovenia. Like dominoes, Croatia, Bosnia, Serbia, and the Republic of Macedonia (FYROM) followed suit. Now refugees became stranded in huge numbers in Athens, and also near the tiny Greek farming hamlet of Idomeni. northern Greece was ill-prepared to handle the needs of this massive bottleneck of humanity. Human suffering again became catastrophic. As humanitarians and medical relief volunteers, our missions abruptly changed too.

We moved our operations from Lesvos to the northern Mainland of Greece where the refugees had become stranded. As before in Lesvos, we encountered overwhelming human needs. The smaller NGO's followed the leads of the larger NGOs in our best efforts to complement their services. Like bricks and mortar, over the next two months, we systematically built up our infrastructure by overcoming organizational rivalries and working together. We were just beginning to get a handle on these human needs: not only in health care, but also in food, shelter, clothing distribution, sanitation, schools, mosques and churches. In terms of medical services, we collectively developed a dental clinic, a women's health program, a chronic-care medicine program, a massive week-long childhood vaccination program, larger sturdier clinic facilities, and better hygiene through more showers, toilets, and feeding centers. And now it is all in the process of being dismantled as we start all over again in the military camps.

Now we are moving on to Part Three. The rules are changing right out from under us, again. There are now about 54-thousand refugees who are stranded in this ever changing limbo here in Greece. The Greek government is moving toward longer-term measures to address the crisis. The smaller gas station camps of BP and Hara were the first to be dismantled. Then on May 24th 2016, authorities began forcibly dismantling the makeshift camp at Idomeni and moving its residents to relocation centers, aka military camps, run by the Greek government. Eko Camp, too, will probably soon be dismantled along with all these improvisational medical and other humanitarian services that volunteers from all around the world have painstakingly developed to support the refugees.

So now, organizations like Salaam Cultural Museum, Kitrinos, and Syrian American Medical Society have to re-invent ourselves again for the third time in less than a year. Our partners in the larger NGOs like Medecins Sans Frontieres, Medecins du Monde, UN High Commission for Refugees, International Committee of the Red Cross, and many others must do the same. There are now new players in the equation, chiefly the Greek military.

It is hard to know at this moment whether these most recent moves to more permanent relocation centers will be better or worse for the refugees. There will probably be those who benefit and those whose hopes perish. We can only pray that these relocation centers will achieve some longer term stability: both for the refugees and for those of us who try our best to provide services for them. But we will continue to do whatever it takes to help: to provide comfort, medical care, shelter, sustenance and to show that some of us in this world, at least, still do care.

© Abdulazez Dukhan

A woman sits in front of the warehouse full of tents in Vasilika Camp, the military camp where nearly 1,500 refugees were relocated from Eko

23
Compassion through Action

Saturday, May 21, 2016.
Chalkidona, Greece
Madi Williamson
(From a Facebook post)
(Madi Williamson is a humanitarian from Washington State volunteering with SCM. She was inspired to travel to Greece to help with the refugee crisis after successful medical missions to the Dominican Republic and founding her own charity to bring soccer equipment to orphans in Africa.)

I HAVEN'T POSTED IN A WHILE, because I have been a bit too busy and over-whelmed. I am re-posting this part because I'm still feeling the same way as before: I'm not a hero. None of us are. But we all have something in us that draws us here to care for other human beings. It takes all shapes and sizes but it's been an amazing thing to witness. Saying goodbye to my teams who have volunteered for SCM, SAMS, and Kitrinos each week is heartbreaking, but meeting all of these wonderful souls with the same common goal really gives me a lift. I feel very fortunate to be here amongst so many big hearts.

I want the world to see the reality of this situation. I'm not a lifesaver nor a hero and I'm not drastically improving the lives of my refugee friends here. I didn't come here to get a new profile picture or to slap it on future job applications. I came here to show these people that I care enough to not pretend that their struggle doesn't exist and to tell them that there are others like me. I want to show them that they aren't alone.

There are very few things that will change their circumstances. You need to educate yourself. Aleppo is being blown off the face of the earth. American and Russian made bullets and bombs are tearing apart innocent people. We literally allow our politicians to get away with murder. You need to vote. You need to demand more from your government and your media. You need to give these people and their struggle the attention they deserve. We are indirectly ruining and ending lives. That's a fact. Humanity is one race and one religion and we do a shitty job taking care of each other. It's not that hard to do.

I'm a strong believer in the power of just showing up. Show up to the polls and the protests. Show up to the disaster zones. Combat media brainwashing by sharing posts from people like me. I know that my voice is powerful because I'm a witness to this chaos and a second-hand witness to the ongoing havoc we have created in the Middle East.

In fifty years, what will you be telling your kids and grandkids when they learn about the biggest mass-migration since WWII? Hopefully you'll be telling them that you stood up for what's right and just, even in a situation where that road was far less traveled.

Sunday, May 29th Sindos, Greece

This week has been the longest and most intense emotional rollercoaster I've ever ridden. Last week, we were given health care responsibilities at a new military camp, or relocation center called Sindos. With the closure of the makeshift camp at Idomeni and the impending closure of the other make-shift camps like Eko which are sure to follow, refuges are now being moved to places like Sindos as an intermediate solution. Our medical teams of SCM/SAMS and Kitrino are moving along right with the refugees. The speed at which international volunteers try their best to create a loving community never ceases to amaze me.

But here at Sindos, right now, the sanitation is horrible and the food is bland. This is a nightmare for anyone trying to manage their blood sugar or women who are pregnant or nursing. There is a lot to do to build infra-structure back to a functional standard.

The shelter here at Sindos is a step up from living in a tent in the muddy fields of Idomeni. But it's still no place for children, or for the medically vulnerable people we've identified here. We have two patients who need dialysis. Finding ways to provide that for them has consumed so much of my heart and energy. I don't just want them to get dialysis; I want them to get the best treatment possible. Dialysis is grim, even in America where you can pay your way to the best treatment.

But following their journey has broken my heart. I can only cling to the hope that the refugees at least know that, while it seems like the world is against them, we are in their corner. And so went my Monday. Call the ambulance, give the patients money for the cab, and wait. They don't make it home until 1 am the next day.

On Tuesday, I meet my new best friend in Sindos. He's the sweetest baby I've ever laid eyes on. And even though he comes to us in the midst of an allergy fit, sneezing and goopy, I still fall in love with him. He was born with a disability and he and his family are going to face a lifetime of struggles. I get the ball rolling on getting him and his family to a safe place where he can be raised with the support he needs. For the time being, I watch his beautiful mama dote on him in spite of people staring at him and even going so far as to ask, "what's wrong with the baby?" It's a regular heartbreak, but her strength and love for her baby is contagious.

On Wednesday, one of my other new friends in Sindos falls ill and I spend the day on a wild goose chase calling all of the hospitals in Thessaloniki trying to figure out which emergency room she had been admitted to and what has happened to her. She's fine and is back to her old self, but I am stressed by the experience of not being able to find her. My Ippocrateo Hospital experience left me devastated and helpless. (Picture every hospital in bad horror movies: dim and broken lights, unattended patients staggering around the halls or leaning against the wall looking unwell, questionable hygiene, and not a single member of the staff to be found.) I hate feeling out of control, especially when I feel that a person has trusted me with their health and well-being.

Just when I am thinking that my week can't get any crazier, Thursday rolls along. At Eko camp, we are briefed about a family whose son is sick, very sick. The unconfirmed diagnosis has been muscular dystrophy. His oxygen saturations are low. Mohammad and Hassan are working around the clock to support the family and to try and keep the boy stable.

Although aware of their grim situation, I keep my distance because selfishly, I am scared. I am scared that I'll care too much. The family is finally brought to the attention of the amazing Dr Matt Keller from Switzerland. I know they are in good hands based on the extent of my interactions with him.

I have been playing with the youngest daughter outside of their tent in front of our mobile clinics, seeing her wave occasionally at mom or dad. All of Thursday is a whirlwind of activity around tent number seven. Discussions are being held on everything from transporting the child to a hospital in Thessaloniki to funeral arrangements should the child not make it. There is nothing worse than contemplating the funeral of a child.

All day Thursday, I feel like my heart is being torn to pieces. Not only do I inevitably come to care about this family, but I love my colleagues with all my heart. They are caretakers and guardian angels. Seeing this child's condition tears them up inside and in turn it destroys me. But then, just an hour before we are due to shut down our clinic and leave for the day, Mohammad is given the green light from contacts in Switzerland. Dr Matt has gotten the approval to relocate the family to Basel where the boy and his sister will receive the care that they need. The only catch is moving a child who is so sick and unstable. While we are excited and thrilled, we know that the journey is going to be very dangerous for the boy. Even if they do manage to keep him stable, there is a chance that the airport or the pilot will deem him unfit to fly.

And so ensues the most stressful twenty-four hours of my life, as I do my part to help with the coordination. I will this boy to live. On Friday, with Swiss visas in hand, Mohammad manages to convince the pilot to let them fly. Three bottles of oxygen and a whole lot of stress later, the family arrives in their new home. They'll receive all of the financial, medical, and social support that they'll need. Honestly I still can't believe it. I still think it's all just a dream.

You don't know inspiration until you've seen the way this team works: Mohammad the Palestinian-American Nurse Anesthetist student from Chicago . . . a tireless activist and our fearless leader during this endeavor; Hassan one of our in-camp translators; Dr Matt our Swiss doctor with critical connections back home; and Petros our much valued Greek-speaking volunteer who deals with the Greek authorities. None of this would have been possible without each member of this team contributing their specific set of skills to the overall task.

I can't express my gratitude. Sometimes this work is isolating, it feels like the world has forgotten about our refugee friends here and the struggles that are their daily reality. The passion and dedication that these people on our team demonstrate on behalf of someone in need restores my faith in the beauty and the goodness of humans.

I've learned a lot about friendship and love during my time here. I've come to care deeply for people whom I can't even have a conversation with because of language barriers. I've eaten their food, danced their dance, braided their hair, bandaged up their boo-boos, held their babies, and we smile and laugh together on a daily basis. For those whom I can talk to, the fact that we share this experience and ride this insane roller coaster together has made us friends for life. I love my teammates too, like I love my family: deeply and unconditionally.

The next challenge we will soon face is the evacuation of the camp surrounding Eko Gas Station near Polykastro. Idomeni camp is no more. I'm not ready to go back to Idomeni yet and see what has become of a place that was once bustling with activity. It wasn't ideal, but it was a place I came to enjoy and appreciate. It was a phase that we all experienced together.

For my friends and family back home, I want you to know how much my time here is changing me and for those of you who I've met over here, I want you to know how much the days I've spent with you mean to me. This isn't easy work, but it's very valuable work. I can't presently imagine my life being any other way. Thank you to my Eko and SAMS/SCM family and to all of the parties involved. It's been a tough week and there are many challenges ahead, but we've been handed a hell of a test and we nailed it. Well done.

May 30, 2016

It's not over. The continued struggle of refugees is my daily reality. They flee war and bear the physical and emotional wounds of the horrors they have witnessed. They trade their freedom and their home, their families and their communities, in exchange for their lives and end up in limbo, tossed back and forth between locations, beyond their control. They are treated like pawns; their lives are being tossed around in turmoil like some sort of sick game.

These are human beings. They wouldn't make this journey and become homeless if they had any other better choice. Open your eyes and then open your heart. This has to end. I can't say this enough: this is the largest human-itarian crisis of our generation. Where do you stand? This isn't an issue we can just throw money at; this issue needs activism and compassion. Stand up for these people with your voice, your actions and your votes, not just your wallet. Don't let this agony go on in vain. Demand more for these people.

24
Evacuation Days

June 2016
Macedonian Greece
Madi Williamson

OUR MEDICAL RELIEF TEAMS have been sharing the same hotel with the Greek riot police. The police buses load and unload out back right under my bathroom window and the officers climb the stairs under the window next to my bed. On a warm day, when I have all of the windows open, I hear them when they change shifts at 7:30 am and when they come home at night around 9:00 pm.

The afternoon shift mingles with our mix of aid workers, tourists, and locals sitting in the bar and restaurant area of the hotel. The few police that I have engaged with over breakfast or during a football game come from Athens. They are generally guarded when sharing their political beliefs, some of them more open than others. Some of them silently stare in shock at this outspoken American girl who obsesses over football and asks a few too many questions. Over time, I am developing a good relationship with some others of these Greek riot police.

On two occasions, I have even exchanged a smile and a nod with them when I see them at work in Idomeni along the train tracks that lead towards the double-barbed-wire-fenced border, complete with no-man's-land of the Former Yugoslav Republic of Macedonia (FYROM). In this line of work, we take things day by day, sometimes hour by hour or minute by minute. We don't have the luxury of foresight. Things can change in an instant. As a rule of thumb, I try to be friendly with everyone; because in all fairness, it doesn't help the situation to be enemies. We're all stuck in the various circumstances that we find ourselves in and we're all reacting in the best way that we can with the different mandates and resources that we have.

BP and Hotel Hara were the first two camps to be evacuated. These smaller camps sit within spitting distance of the highway border crossing. My colleagues and I, who have US, EU and UK passports, can cross this border with relative ease by spending fifty Euros every two weeks to take a carload full of aid workers back and forth between FYROM and Greece as often as we want. Meanwhile the refugees are trapped here and can go no further unless they pay smugglers exorbitant prices to get them across illegally.

In March, I spent a total of fifteen minutes in BP and Hara camps during my first day here on the ground. Due to my limited exposure, I have no emotional ties to these places. For me, these camps seemed to lack the cohesive community spirit that I experienced and was a part of due to my strong association with Eko Camp and some pockets of Idomeni Camp. I didn't grieve when BP and Hara were taken down. That evening, I watched the European football matches with a few of the riot police officers and my medical team and then closed my window when I heard the noisy bus roll in for their nightly shift change.

We all knew the evacuation of Eko was coming. After BP and Hara, Idomeni was dismantled. The photos made me sick. I am of mixed race, the daughter and granddaughter of Japanese-Americans on my mother's side. During WWII, my grandfather's entire family was rounded up and placed in the American internment camps simply because of their race. (Some German-Americans were rounded up based on their political beliefs, but their numbers were miniscule. All Japanese-Americans were summarily sent to camps, except those who served in the US armed forces.) I knew how this was going to end. With all of their worldly possessions packaged up and placed in front of large tourist buses, the scene was sickeningly familiar.

Now it's almost seventy-four years on from the day my family stood by a bus with whatever they could carry. They were waiting to be taken to "Camp Harmony," a renovated space in and around horse stalls at the Puyallup Fairgrounds in Washington State. Now here stand the oppressed once again while the world looks on in silence. Different times, different circumstances, but at what point do we learn that there are right and wrong ways to handle this? When do we learn that all humans can and must be treated with basic dignity?

The residents of Idomeni have now been dispersed to various camps around Thessaloniki operated by the Greek military and police. These new relocation centers or military camps are located down winding dirt roads. The drive to these places is full of despair. It feels as though you are driving to the ends of the earth; the perfect place to relocate people you wish to keep silent-out of sight and out of mind.

June 13th, at 6:00 am, I get the text: Eko is being evacuated. I was asleep, and missed the earlier-than-normal morning deployment of all of the police buses. A doctor from the medical team and I meet in the lobby and then try to make our way up to Eko Camp to say our goodbyes. The fear of never seeing these people again shakes me to my core, with an overwhelming feeling of helplessness. The first photos come in on my smart phone. People I have come to know and love are standing in front of buses, or taking pictures of the tent that they have called home for the past three months. They are taking selfies with friend and bidding tearful goodbyes. I long to see that place full of life and love one more time before it meets the fate of the camps that fell before it and it is bulldozed to the ground.

The highways are closed. The Greek officials clearly do not want anyone interfering with the evacuation operations, which is understandable from their perspective. So we're forced to turn around. Bitter disappointment doesn't even begin to cover it. While I have faith I will see my Eko family again, I am not sure where or when or how. I feel a deep sense of sadness and guilt knowing that they will have to go through the dehumanizing evacuation process without my show of support and my previous promise that I will find them, no matter where they are taken.

Instead of going to Eko, we turn around and head to our other work at the new relocation centers. These are where refugees who have previously been evacuated (first voluntarily and then by force) are now living. The new camps have stricter regulations concerning which NGOs are allowed to come and go. Generally, I am in agreement with this. Sometimes stricter measures must be taken to maintain a sense of order and to keep people safe. But for many weeks as we were trying to plan for transitioning to the camps we didn't know if SCM or the Syrian American Medical Society would be granted access to these camps controlled by the Greek military.

On we go with our day here at Karamanlis Camp and the ups and downs that come with aid work. It is harder to concentrate today, while thinking about the pandemonium that our friends are experiencing an hour north with the dismantling of Eko Camp. I call some ambulances, I meet with the police. I hold my favorite little baby and talk with his lovely mama. Life goes on here, but my heart is heavy. You never learn how to grieve in complete chaos and uncertainty. In the evening after work, I have a drink and dinner in my room. I sit and look over the photos, feeling sick.

"We've been assigned a tent number. They refer to us as a number. There aren't enough toilets, this is not a place for humans." "I'm so sorry, my friend. I'm sorry that this has happened to you."

I sit and hold my phone numbly for nearly an hour and then, like clock-work, the police bus pulls in and the exhausted officers trek up the steps. I think of my police friends and the laughs we have shared together and how they have proudly showed me photos of their children and bragged about their football club being the best in all the land. They have occasionally bought me a beer. They have thoughtfully answered my pestering questions about what was being said in Greek on the TV news, or what they thought about this whole mess that we are in. Like everyone else, they're just living their lives as best they can with no malicious intentions. If anything, they seem to have a little bit of guilt or even fear. I sink down on my bed as my head spins. I feel the comfort of the soft mattress and cool sheets on my skin. I think of my refugee friends, curled up in another strange place, uprooted once again. The injustice of it is agonizing.

Tears fall on the sheets while combat boots pound the steps underneath my window. It feels as though everything is falling to the ground around me. The world seems like an exponentially more complex place than we always thought it would be when we were young. Sometimes there are no sides. There are no rights, wrongs, winners or losers. Sometimes we are just helpless; how fragile we are.

25
Class Dismissed

June 13, 2016
Eko Camp
Mohammad J Deen

A LOUD KNOCKING ON MY DOOR at 6 am startles me from my sleep. "Are you awake? Wake up, wake up! They are evacuating Eko Camp; the police are at Eko right now! We have to go! Now!"

6:10 am: "Mohammad, do you know where the police are taking us? Do you know where we are going? Why are they surrounding the camp with military buses? And why have they shut down the roads? They have told us that we have until seven am, and then they will start to clear out the refugee camp and force us into buses."

6:12 am: Still trying to wake up, I'm thinking, "Maybe this is a nightmare . . . maybe this isn't real." In the weeks leading up to this day before my scheduled departure back to the US, I have spent many nights sleeping in Eko camp as the lone member of the night shift for the medical teams. On my last night, I decided to sleep in the room that I rented near the refugee camp so I can pack my things in preparation for departure. I also needed to pack up extra medications I had stockpiled for my night watch duties and return them to the medical team warehouse. I have been living in the refugee camp for a while and I have almost forgotten what it's like to sleep indoors.

6:20 am, after arriving back at Eko Camp: A refugee approaches me. "Mohammad, you need to pretend that you're a refugee. They're arresting all of the volunteers who are not leaving the camp. If you need to hide, hide in our tent!" I am making my way to the tent when a police officer approaches me.

Police Officer: "Hey, I need to see your passport!"

Me: "I am an American volunteer with one of the medical teams in the camp."

Police Officer: "You can't be here right now. We will take them to a different camp. The buses are coming soon."

Petros Tsetris, our Greek volunteer comes to my defense. "He needs to stay. He is taking care of the ambulances and is here to assist if someone gets sick or hurt. He needs to be here." His plea works, and I am able to stay.

7:00 am: The Greek police begin to search the school that we have set up in the camp. They begin to tear down some of the tents that were set up by volunteers like the Nurture Project tent that has provided a space for women and babies, and the Eko Kitchen tent where volunteers come to cook meals to supplement the food that is distributed by Doctors without Borders. They're looking for volunteers trying to hide among the refugees and they want to make sure no refugees are hiding.

7:30 am: I am feeling overwhelmed and in total shock over what is happening. About ten police buses are now surrounding the camp and over one hundred officers are swarming in to make sure that everyone is evacuated. People are being loaded on to the buses as the police sweep through to make sure the volunteers are gone. I decide to walk through the camp.

I walk around to each camp site, checking on my sick patients and making sure that they're *ok*. As I walked towards the center of the camp I notice a group of men dancing one final traditional *dabke*, dance. They hold hands around a man playing a string instrument and dance through their present struggle and dance through the pain. What other choices do they have?

I join them for a moment, but then I have to leave to watch from a distance. I have to leave the circle because I can't stop myself from tearing up.

Once again, these people who have become my friends are being told where to go. They are being sent to an unknown place,: herded up like sheep and forgotten. This is very hard for me to watch. When I arrived at Eko camp three months ago, they were settled. I have never in my life experienced or witnessed the displacement of a population until this day, and it stings. Watching children collect the very few toys they have and put them into bags, and watching families round up the very few clothing articles that they have. It's not what I have envisioned.

10 am: Buses pull in to the gas station and people start boarding. I have never had to say so many goodbyes all at once before. This was supposed to be my last day in camp before returning to the USA. It was supposed to be a good day. Yesterday, I had planned on throwing a party for my English class. I have been teaching this class daily for eight weeks in addition to my medical obligations. This isn't how it was supposed to be. As I began to cry, the refugees notice me in tears and one tries to comfort me. He has been a student of mine. He has frequently told me, "Mohammad, I will make you proud. I

am going to go to Sweden. I will finish my education and come visit you in America." I break down even more as soon as I see him walking towards me. He wants me to stop crying. He wipes tears off of my face and says, "I will be seeing you soon, my teacher."

I have to ask myself, "Why am I crying? I have gone through nothing compared to these people who have become my friends." I think it's the shock; the shock of seeing an event like this take place with your own eyes. My friends are being told where to go while the tents that they built, the school and kitchen they had formed, the community that they had grown to accept is all being demolished. Once again, they are being displaced. Refugees on the move, again!

1:00 pm: The refugees board the buses, filling them one at a time. The highway leading south towards Thessaloniki has been closed off and no one is allowed to enter or exit the refugee camp without approval from the police. Each bus has a police escort to its final destination, which will be a new longer term refugee camp approximately seventy kilometers away.

As the camp is being systematically evacuated, I stand by the ambulances that have served as our clinics for all of this time feeling completely alienated and despondent. I am approached by the same police officer who had asked for my papers earlier. "Why are you crying? What connection do you have with these people?"

"What connection?" I ask incredulously. "How can you be so cold? These people have lost everything. They have nothing; and here you are coming to take them away. You're herding them up like a bunch of sheep. These people did not want to end up in your country. They were just trying to pass by and got stuck. It's not their fault that their home country is being destroyed. What would you do if your family were in danger? Would you watch them die or would you pack your things and go? How would you feel if the world watched you suffer without doing a thing? Again and again we make them feel even worse, rounding them up and taking them to another unknown place."

He looks at me and responds, "It's not me, my friend. It's the people above me. I can't do anything about this." As he says these words, a young refugee girl comes to say goodbye. She's in tears as she tries to thank me. But she is so choked up; she can't even echo the words, "*shukran*," which means, "thank you" in Arabic, as she approaches me.

She has also been one of my students in the English class. I remember her because she has been so shy. But I have been pushing her, and she has never given up, always smiling. But now she's drowning in tears as she approaches me to say one last goodbye. At this point, the expressions of the Greek police officer have changed. Maybe he has a daughter who is her age. Maybe he sees the connection I have with the refugees here. He finally says, "You can stay here until we clear out the camp, we will not bother you. My supervisors know who you are. But this camp is done and it will be cleared out." And with that, he walks away.

5:00 pm: This evacuation day has been one of the hardest days of my life. I have never cried so much in one day. The camp is now empty. The refugees have grabbed what little they have. Several of my friends are waving goodbye to me from the windows of the buses.

Before the final bus leaves, a group of my students who I have been teaching for the past two months comes to say their goodbyes. Once again, I can't stop myself from tearing up. Another one of my students wipes the tears off my face and says, "I will see you again. You will come and visit me and watch me give a presentation in English in my new university one day." And to that I say, "I'll be at your wedding, too!"

They're very motivated. They want to move on with their lives. This is why my class went from five students to forty in nearly a week with refugees walking in from camps eight km away to attend the class.

8:30 pm: I make my final walk through the Eko camp. This time, it's empty of the people who had given it life for the past four months. No one is left except some of the volunteers collecting their supplies. I walk into the school, the same school where I had taught English daily for two months. It's been a place full of people and activity; happiness and joy. But this time, it's empty. I'm the only one left standing here. My last day here did not turn out as I had planned; instead, it was an evacuation of the entire camp.

I never had the chance to say, "Class Dismissed!," because before I could do so, the entire Eko Camp was dismissed instead.

Eko Camp following it's demolition in June 2016.

IV
Reflections

26
Medical Care in Military Camps

September 2, 2016
Back home in New Jersey
Kelly Griffin MD
(Dr Griffin is a critical care physician from California, now living in New Jersey, and working in New York. She volunteered with SAMS.)

How do I write about my time in Greece? I don't know where to begin. The logistics? The bearing-witness? The guilt in leaving? The anger and frustration that we feel, let alone the refugees, at the fact that our voices are being collectively ignored by the whole world? I sit and stare at my computer screen. I feel speechless . . . furious . . . unspeakably sad. We can't be speechless though, we need to speak as loudly as possible—so I will try.

In early June, 2016, I went to northern Greece, up near the Macedonian border. The opportunity for me to volunteer in a medical clinic in one of the refugee camps was a sort of unbelievable confluence of circumstance and incredibly supportive family, friends, and colleagues. I found an NGO—the Syrian American Medical Society, or SAMS—dedicated to helping Syrians both within Syria and those living as refugees. When the opportunity presented itself and circumstances allowed, I leapt at the chance to volunteer in one of their clinics.

I had watched the horrifying news coverage of the Syrian civil war, at that point already 5+ years on and counting. I cried watching refugees crammed into overcrowded rafts attempting the dangerous passage to Greece, desperate to reach safety for themselves and for their children. I cried harder seeing lifeless bodies pulled from the water and innumerable orange life jackets stacked on the beach. I have young children. I would have been doing the same flight for life if I were in their shoes.

When I got there, the refugees had been moved from a few large, informal camps primarily at Idomeni, (which at one point had several thousand refugees) into smaller, "official" camps run by the Greek military. The SAMS clinics had only been operating in these new camps for two weeks, and things were still quite hectic. The camps themselves were abandoned factory buildings that had been very quickly converted into shelters. There were rows of military-type tents set up within these giant factory buildings. Each tent was assigned to a family. Features of the camp also included portable toilets along with communal sinks, lots of mud and mosquitoes. The SAMS clinics were a little different in each camp, but basically they were little rooms in corners of these big buildings.

For the most part, the medical issues we saw were not especially complicated: diarrhea, fevers, coughs, overwhelming mosquito bites, infected mosquito bites, lacerations on arms and legs, etc. The close living quarters and poor sanitation at the camps made contagious illnesses spread quickly, so we saw many of the same illnesses repeatedly. There was a group of Spanish Ob/Gyns driving around to different camps for prenatal exams and fetal ultrasounds, there was also a rotating ophthalmologist and rumors of a dental group. Patients who needed to be seen by other specialists were referred to local clinics, but the waits were long and the transport was not always easy to arrange.

Anyone who was really sick—and we did have a few of those—were sent by ambulance to one of the local hospitals. Even this was not totally straightforward. The military police running the camps were uniformly quick and helpful to call ambulances for us, but there was no guarantee of a way back to the camps for the refugees. The Greek public transportation system is difficult to navigate if you don't speak the language: a gross understatement. Parents had to find care from their tent-neighbors for the kids remaining at camp. There are also no widely-available language translation services available in Greek hospitals. I am spoiled having become used to on-line translation services back home in American hospitals. I literally cannot imagine doing my job caring for patients who speak various languages without these services. So Arabic, Farsi or Kurdish speaking patients could show up at the closest hospital. If it wasn't very clear why they were there, the workup would become immensely more complicated, and potentially incomplete. That said, I had some very good interactions with Greek physicians by phone—calling to clarify our concerns or give updates—and the few I spoke with went to great lengths to try to find translators and provide high-quality care.

All that said, the medicine wasn't the striking thing about being there. The people were. These lovely, warm, heart-broken people could be my friends and neighbors at home. They could be me. They are me. The injustice of their situation agonizes me still. These are educated, kind, family-oriented people whose cities fell apart. The skies literally fell. They fled, to a person, with either physical or emotional scars, often both. We—the world—collectively turned our backs. We watched, momentarily horrified, until the next news cycle. These were pregnant women . . . young children . . . teenagers . . . old folks. They are all now living in tents, on the filthy floors of abandoned factories, in mosquito-ridden fields surrounded by rusty wire and wild dogs. And many of the authorities seem to feel that this is enough. It isn't. It simply isn't.

Coming back from Greece, I have been going through the stages of "reverse culture shock": at first, so angry, so ready to be an advocate. And later on I am feeling sort of numb. At the beginning, I slammed my Facebook page with posts to raise awareness and ways to try to help. My wonderful, well-meaning circle-of-friends have been endlessly supportive and encouraging.

There was a boy I met in Greece, a six-year-old, who had been shot in the head a year earlier and had bullet fragments retained in his brain and a large hole in his skull, pulsatile brain visible just under his skin. I came home and found a neurosurgeon willing to volunteer his surgical services, the hospital willing to donate the care, but the logistics of his being granted a medical visa to come to the US for care are almost impossible to overcome. It just all feels hopeless and small.

How many more children have to sit on an orange ambulance chair, covered in blood and dust, in shock and crying; making the global rounds as the latest face of this tragedy? How long do families have to sleep in camps without registration by the UNHCR, without education for their children and themselves, and in forced total dependence on a kindhearted but overwhelmed Greek government?

It's been months now, and I still think of the friends I met and the patients I cared for countless times during every day as I try to fall asleep every single night. I am not a politician. I don't know how to solve the Syrian crisis. I do know that barrel bombs should not be dropped on cities. Hospitals should not be targets. Safety corridors for evacuations and humanitarian aid should be maintained.

I am going back in November. I feel a bit mixed about going. This has been hard on me. That alone is reason for me to go—it has been hard on me, and I have a choice. I will be there for a week. I'll return to a safe and comfortable home, a great job, and a loving family. For me to say that working in the camps for one little week was hard. Imagine how hard it is on the people living it. So I am going back, heartbreak and frustration be damned. It feels like so little, but it's one of the only things I can do. Shouting from the rooftops about the Syrian crisis hasn't seemed to dramatically alter the global conscience, but maybe this one little thing that I can do is something. There were refugee friends that I made, people to whom I told, "I'll be back." For people who have met innumerable broken promises, maybe this one small thing is something: a promise I have to keep.

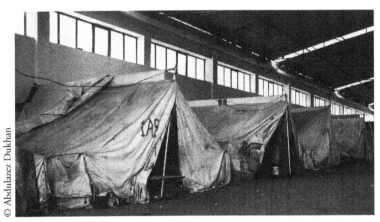

Family tents inside of Vasilika camp, home to over 1,000 refugees after they were evacuated from Eko Camp in the north and taken to a more permanent location to await the asylum process.

27
Returning from Lesvos

February 1, 2016
Back Home on Bainbridge Island, Washington, USA
Timothy Spenser
(Tim has a degree in Political Economy and Social Movements. He is from Washington State and now living in Colorado. He was a humanitarian volunteer on Lesvos for SCM. His mother's paternal grandparents emigrated to the USA from Lesvos.)

ONE DAY I AM KNEE-DEEP IN THE AEGEAN SEA, helping people off an overcrowded dinghy onto a pebbly beach. Prayers are offered. Cigarettes are promptly lit. Dry clothing is distributed. Tea is brewed and ladled out. Sodden family members hold each other. They breathe sighs of relief, having made the crossing from Turkey safely, and they also shed tears for the shattered countries they have left behind and for loved ones who have been lost. Salt, steam, smoke, and sunlight mix in the morning air, cool with the approach of winter. This is the shore of the Greek island of Lesvos. The skeletons of wrecked fishing boats and the rubber skins of deflated zodiacs testify to the hundreds of thousands of people who have arrived on these beaches in the last six months. The neon-orange of life jackets discarded in the sand seems to set fire to the whole coastline.

A few days later I am making a sea voyage of my own, this time on the large ferry from Seattle to Bainbridge Island, Washington, my hometown. The distance the ferry travels is actually greater than that between the north coast of Lesvos, where most refugees make landfall, and Turkey. Unlike the people who make that crossing, I do not have to fear that this vessel will capsize, that we will be cast adrift when its engines die mid-passage, or that the coast guard will spot us and turn us back from the hope of the further shore. My eyes unconsciously scan the green waves of the Puget Sound for refugee boats.

At the beginning of December 2015, my mom and I spent two weeks on Lesvos volunteering with the Salaam Cultural Museum (SCM), an aid organization based in Seattle that has coordinated medical missions to the Greek coast since the end of last summer. Neither of us are medical professionals. We don't know Arabic or any of the other languages spoken by the refugees streaming across the water from Turkey. All we had to offer as volunteers was our drive to be of service to others and our willingness to make some small sacrifices in order to do so.

While we were in Greece, our friends and family were able to follow our volunteer activities through social media. Many more people in our community learned about the work we had been doing with SCM. Shortly after returning to the US, we were interviewed by local news media about our experiences. The response elicited by our appearance on KIRO 7 television has been overwhelmingly positive. Friends and acquaintances have expressed interest, encouragement, gratitude, and pride. Some are now planning their own trips to Greece.

During our time on Lesvos, my mom and I were able to witness and participate modestly in a story that needs to be shared, discussed, and reflected upon deeply. Unsurprisingly, the short segment, which aired on the evening news, failed to convey the messages we hoped to raise in all their breadth and depth. But after all, the mainstream news media's role these days is to entertain, not to inform. Sure, doing justice to the story of the refugee crisis requires wading into a morass of complex geopolitical problems, which would be difficult to tackle in under three minutes. Nonetheless, after two weeks of immersion in one of the great humanitarian disasters of our time, we had insights to share which, disappointingly, ended up not making it into the final broadcast. It's been a little over a month since we returned to the United States, enough time to turn things over again and again in my mind, and finally to put into words the things I want to say about what I saw and did in Greece.

First, I'd like to put the contribution that my mom and I made as volunteers into perspective, and to give credit to everyone who has given so much more than we have. The experience we shared on Lesvos was far less demanding and intense than it might have been had we arrived at a different time or stayed longer.

The weeks we spent in early-to-mid-December volunteering coincided with a pronounced decrease in the volume of refugees coming from Turkey. This downturn was caused in part by uncertainty surrounding a deal struck at the end of November 2015 between Turkey and the European Union. Turkey received more than three billion Euros. It also was able to resurrect the discussion around its accession to the EU in exchange for enacting measures designed to stem the flow of people into Europe, including stricter border enforcement

The threat of winter weather also contributed to the lull. October saw refugees landing on the beaches of Lesvos by the thousands on a daily basis. Volunteers were kept running from beach to beach from dawn until well past midnight. By contrast, on the heaviest days in early December we welcomed just a few hundred people ashore, and those mostly with the benefit of daylight. Additionally, when we arrived, there were more resources, more volunteers, and more emergency response infrastructure on Lesvos than there had been just weeks before, all of which lightened our burden considerably. And from what we can tell, the situation has become more challenging again since our departure, with persistent rain and cold temperatures making the crossing that much more dangerous.

Other volunteers, both with SCM and other aid organizations, have made much greater commitments of time and effort than either my mom or I were able to manage. Some have been on Lesvos since the summer, when the number of refugee arrivals began to reach unmanageable levels and before there was any kind of coordinated international response. Those volunteers are responsible for creating, from scratch, much of the aid infrastructure, which currently serves refugees on Lesvos. Teams of lifeguards from Greece and Spain, also volunteering their time, put their own safety at risk to help bring refugee boats safely to shore. Many other volunteers have given more than a month of their lives serving people in need. By comparison, our contribution seems very modest indeed.

Second, the awful scale of the disaster unfolding in the Aegean needs to be emphasized again and again. No aid workers on Lesvos endure hardships or make sacrifices, which approach comparison with the suffering and loss known by the refugees themselves who come ashore in Greece. The crossing is a nexus where a host of global catastrophes such as civil war, foreign military intervention, inter—and intrareligious conflict, political corruption, economic marginalization, etc., meet, compound and get fused momentarily into a single great tragedy in the crucible of an unseaworthy dinghy. Those of us waiting on the beach can only wrap welcoming arms and warming emergency blankets around the survivors.

How to truly wrap our minds around the enormity of their heartbreak? The reality is so ugly, so horrific. The risk I see is that this story becomes focused on the compassionate volunteers rather than the people in need whom they are helping, that this becomes just another way of looking away from the depth of the calamity. We should absolutely celebrate the love, the selfless service, the raw common humanity that manifests whenever a boat arrives from Turkey, but we've got to put it all into perspective as a footnote to the true tragic history. In the midst of embracing someone who has just defied death to make it to European soil, you know and they know that the moment is only a brief reprieve on a path of near-continuous personal and communal hardship. It's crucial that we not lose sight of that bigger, darker picture.

Finally, there are reflections which have only had time to crystallize fully in the month since we came back home. Absorbing the weight of my experiences in Greece, learning to walk with it, to carry it back with me to the United States, has been a mental and emotional challenge. Guilt is there. Guilt for my ability to drop in and out of other peoples' suffering. Guilt for the ease with which I can cross borders and oceans. Guilt for not being on the beach anymore, when I know the crisis is only becoming more dire by the day and help is still needed.

On Lesvos, I was able to directly and immediately offer real assistance to people in need. If I had more time and resources, I'd go back in a heartbeat. Renouncing that face-to-face contact is painful. Returning to the familiar routines of home feels like a betrayal. The real betrayal, though, would be to accept that distance equals powerlessness. In fact, opportunities to be involved with the refugee crisis exist right here in America. Foremost among these is the imperative to be a voice against the tide of small-mindedness that would seek to block refugees from coming to this country.

We are mistaken if we think that, because oceans lie in between, the refugee crisis doesn't touch us in the United States. It's clear that our culture is being tested by this humanitarian disaster. Will America live up to its own self-image as a haven for downtrodden and oppressed people, or will it succumb to the demon of Islamophobia? This country's history is already blighted by examples of bigotry, injustice, ignorance, and tolerance for hateful acts. Will we allow another ugly chapter to be written, one in which we close our doors and our hearts against masses of people fleeing death in search of a better life for themselves and their children because of how they choose to worship?

I've had the opportunity to interact directly with people who, because of their religion or perceived religion, are being painted with the brush of violent extremism by politicians and pundits. They are heroes, putting everything on the line for the sake of a brighter future. Perhaps the most important service I can do for them is to speak up for openness, inclusivity, and the oneness of humankind here at home. I am thankful to share this country with Muslims. It is an immeasurable blessing to live in a society made up of people of many faiths. I want to continue living in such a society. We are strengthened by diversity, not threatened. We should welcome anyone in need, not in spite of their religion, but in celebration of it. And we must be vocal and proactive in the defense of our fellow Americans, Muslim or otherwise, when they are threatened by bigotry, hatred, and exclusion.

The process of putting these impressions into words has been painfully slow. What a test, to distill a coherent message from an experience, which continues to challenge me daily with unresolvable questions. Others have done it better than I. What I've shared is incomplete, mostly because my own thinking still has a long way to go. But the best way to honor the people that I was briefly privileged to serve on Lesvos is to share something of what I saw and something of what it made me think and feel, and to do it in my own words. If I've been able to add some depth or detail to the picture, some complication to the story, then my purpose has been served. I encourage anyone who can find the time and the resources to go see what is happening in Greece for themselves. Be a witness. Lend a hand. Get your heart broken.

28
Humanitarian Work
with Refugees

Reach for the sky... a young girl plays in the fields behind Vasilika Camp, on the outskirts of Thessaloniki, Greece.

November 7, 2016
Macedonian Region, northern Greece
Rasha Abousalem
(Rasha Abousalem is Palestinian-American with a major in International Criminal Justice, with concentrations in human rights and refugees. She has been to Greece multiple times with SCM during the previous year. She returns once again with SCM as a humanitarian volunteer.)

ONCE AGAIN, I HAVE RETURNED TO NORTHERN GREECE four days ago. I have been away from those I've come to regard as my family for about two months now. I have been gone twice as long as I had originally planned. This is not my first time in Greece, nor my first time in dealing with those who have been displaced by war. This time, I am returning for a long-term opportunity. I have quit my job, but most painfully, I have left my husband and dogs behind.

My first time here in the eastern Mediterranean in response to the Syrian refugee crisis was when I packed my five bags of donations in June 2014. I wandered around Jordan from one illegal camp site to another, finally landing in the UN run Za'atari refugee camp. I actually met my current husband in a sand-covered tent when I translated for him during my stay. Considering we had since married, now that I look back, I realize I've been quite the busy one during our first 1.5 years of marriage, bouncing around from one refugee crises site to another.

In September of 2015, I headed to Lesvos and then Idomeni in Greece. By January 2016, I was in Calais, France working with refugees stranded in "The Jungle" who were trying to cross the English Channel to the UK. By the end of April 2016, I was back in Idomeni. About three weeks after returning to the US, I turned right around and headed back to northern Greece in June. I returned again by the end of August and now, two months later, I find myself sitting here again in the same room that I've come to know as my second home.

I first arrived in Jordan back in the summer of 2014 to face, for the first time, a new reality. *Za'atari*, the only legal camp in Jordan, is run by the UNHCR. Many decided to leave and start their own smaller camps; but every so often, the Jordanian army would arrive and place them back in the UN camp. No matter which camp, the men's egos seemed to be hit the hardest. They were not allowed to work. Instead they sat day after day thinking of the lives they used to have not too long ago back in Syria, and how they watched it all destroyed in the blink of an eye. Years of their hard work vanished, as if it never existed at all. As refugees in Jordan, they could not provide even the simplest of necessities for their families. They felt emasculated and humiliated. This would not be the last time I would hear such sentiments.

Next, I arrived on the island of Lesvos in September 2015. I arrived at a time when the media was picking up their coverage of the refugee crises in Europe, and while the numbers of volunteers was still substantially low. All the media outlets would show the same footage: a boat of Syrians wearing life vests arriving on the shores of Lesvos and the refugees stumbling their way to dry land. Needless to say, what I saw within the first fifteen minutes of arriving to the shores of Skala Sikaminias on the northern coast left me speechless.

I met an Athenian police officer upon arriving. I was worried about his presence. Was he friend or foe to the refugees, or even to me? Soon I discovered the answer. I had no idea where to go to find these rafts of people arriving, so I hesitantly asked him, fearing that maybe he would stop me from going. His answer caught me off guard. "Oh, ok, I am going there now. Just follow me."

So we drove down and pulled onto one side of a narrow dirt road. He told me that the Greek government was sending some police from Athens to stay one month at a time to help the arriving refugees. I was really awe-struck. I had incorrectly assumed that the police would be the ones least helpful to those arriving illegally; but in this case, they were there for support.

Within fifteen minutes of our arrival, we received calls that five boats full of people were arriving imminently. On average, forty to fifty bodies overburdened a raft that is meant to hold a maximum of ten people. One of the boats that was driven by a smuggler left people at the bottom of a steep cliff that we then had to slide down to access.

During the next seven days, I heard endless horror stories: from barrel bombings in Syria, and getting arrested and beaten in Turkey, to smugglers firing their guns into the air to scare the refugees onto the overflowing rafts. The more people on each raft, the more money the smugglers made.

In Greece, the refugees were not just Syrian, but also from other places in the Middle East, as well as South Asia and northern Africa: places that were also suffering from internal conflict.

I'll never forget my second morning. A raft full of Syrian refugees was arriving from the distance. The general rule was, if the people on the raft were wearing bright orange vests, that meant they were Syrian. Other colors indicated people from other countries, such as Afghanistan or Somalia.

The routine was for me to yell in Arabic at the approaching raft to stay calm and not to move too much, so as to not flip the raft. Even from a distance, you can hear the screams and cries of the terrified refugees. As they reached the shore, we would ask to disembark the children first, followed by the elderly and women, and then the men.

After we finished with this one particular boat, a tall man with red hair approached me. "My mother! My mother! She was in a raft that left two hours earlier than mine and I do not see her! I don't know if her boat sank or if she is even still alive!" he hysterically cried to me. A man in his 40's, crying his heart out to me in Arabic, and I have absolutely no idea what to say to him. I told him that the boat most likely returned back to the Turkish shore, which was a mere six miles away in the distance. I never found out if he found his mother, or if she even survived the journey.

Boat after boat, day after day, night after night the refugees arrived. Every boat was full of terrified men, women, and children. I lost count of how many infants I was handed, and how many very pregnant women we'd helped off of the rafts, or how many collapsed upon reaching the shores.

After Lesvos, I flew back to Athens with three other American volunteers. We rented a van and drove over eight hours with seventeen boxes of humanitarian aid to the Greek-Macedonian town of Idomeni. For several hours, we handed out humanitarian aid to those waiting to cross into the Former Yugoslav Republic of Macedonia. At that time, this Macedonian border was open and welcoming. Refugees were still crossing the border successfully on their way to northern Europe. There was a small Red Cross station and two large UN tents. A bus of refugees would arrive, and the people would be assembled into groups, and then numbered. They would receive bread and water; and then they would wait for their numbers to be called before crossing the border.

When I first walked in, I heard someone calling out my name, "Rasha! Rasha!" I looked ahead and saw a young man, who was waiting in the line for his number, waiving at me. It took me a second to remember him as he yelled out, "You remember me from Lesvos several days ago? You helped me off a raft and you joked that we might see each other at the Macedonian border!" I was speechless. We chatted for a while and he even helped us hand out aid as he waited for his group number to be called. And he wasn't the only person I ran into, who just days earlier was stumbling off of a raft. I walked to the border, literally to the invisible line in the dirt that was suddenly the Republic of Macedonia, and would wave my new friends off as they continued their journey toward a new life.

By winter 2015/16, there had been a massive influx of volunteers to Lesvos. Overwhelming humanitarian needs were finally being adequately addressed there. In January, I decided to head to Calais, France, to the refugee camp known as "the Jungle." At the time, I was part of the medical relief agency known as Global First Responder. We led a medical/humanitarian team to the massively underserved camp located by the English Channel. The conditions were beyond horrendous; they were inhumane. Families, single parents, young men, and unaccompanied minors were sleeping mainly in flimsy tents that took a daily beating from the unbearably cold winds coming from the port.

We handed out knit hats and gloves, but we had no shoes to give to the countless people walking around in the cold mud wearing only their flip-flops. Soon, I was getting daily calls of unaccompanied minors arriving at our medical tent for me to deal with. A child who is on their own is bad enough. But within the camp, there was the lingering dark secret of the child sex trafficking industry, a problem that is rampant throughout certain parts of Europe. The youngest unaccompanied child that I met in the camp was a ten year old boy who traveled from Afghanistan. This child made a 3,500 mile journey on his own that took him one month! Sleeping on his own . . . walking on his own . . . spending nights on his own . . . and encountering God knows who; on his own!

Many were startled and naturally wondered why his parents would allow him to take such a dangerous journey. The answer becomes quite clear when one considers the circumstances this child lived in back in his village. Militant groups, such as the Taliban, constantly used child soldiers to do their dirty work, and males were the only kinds of soldiers used. So now, imagine what conditions back home must have been like, such that his parents found it a safer risk for their young boy to leave and travel thousands of miles on his own.

At the end of April, I returned to Greece to provide translation for SCM/SAMS at Idomeni and at a camp known as Eko. By this time, Idomeni was not the same place it had been when I was there seven months before, back in September. Now, the border was slammed shut. In September, Idomeni was covered in vast farmlands and fields. Only hundreds of refugees at a time who were in transit were there for a short period of time before moving on. By April, it was overflowing with thousands of stranded refugees. Small and huge tents of every description fanned out haphazardly in every direction. At one point, there had been up to about 20,000 refugees from all over the world stuck there. I had no idea that I would again see so many of the same volunteers and refugees I had come to know on my previous trip to Greece during the fall and winter of 2015. They would still be there. They would be the same ones that I would again be working so closely with in these camps during the spring and summer of 2016.

Although the Macedonian government blocked the refugees from entering, everyday a rumor would start. That the next day or the day after that, the border would open. Slowly and painfully, with each passing day, people lost hope; and in turn they became angry and desperate.

Can you imagine what it must feel like to know that the only thing separating you from reuniting with your family in Germany is a barbed-wire fence at the Macedonian border? That literally right in front of you is a road that will take you one step closer to asylum? That just days prior to your arrival, this same border was open? The regrets they must have felt for not leaving earlier must have been immeasurable. If only they had left one week earlier, or even just one day, they would not be stuck in this horrible predicament.

After returning home in May, I found myself yearning. I just couldn't get it out of my system. I flew back once again to Greece only three weeks later, after accepting a longer term opportunity. I arrived during the Muslim fasting month of Ramadan in June and started the grueling process of surveying children from tent-to-tent. Speaking with different families, the subject ranged from the years of schooling missed (or absolutely no schooling at all), to mothers literally crying about how desperate they are and how inhumane this situation is. Yet among all the families, there was one common concern: their beloved children.

The vast majority of the children, up to eleven years of age in both camps, had never attended school at all. Because at the time they would have started school back in Syria, the war had begun. Some had received sporadic schooling, mainly in Turkey. This became evident as some of the children were able to speak in rudimentary Turkish as well as their native Arabic or Kurdish. Yet the most amazing thing that I was witnessing was the excitement that these kids expressed at the idea of attending some sort of schooling, no matter how unofficial it was.

Soon I discovered that my work would quickly expand to cover other aspects of camp life. It is an amazing experience to volunteer, no matter where or in what capacity. Regardless of language barriers, you can easily connect, simply with a friendly smile. People know when they are genuinely being helped. They can sense the humbleness and sincerity of volunteers. Yet as someone who speaks Arabic, the main language of those we are helping, it takes the experience to a completely different and many times overwhelming level. There is a deeper connection made, if one allows it so. Yet this can come at a deep emotional cost.

They speak of their struggles: the war, the family and friends they've lost either by death or separation. They speak of the homeland they've loved and watched destroyed before their very eyes. Before I knew it, the tears were streaming down their cheeks; both women and men alike. Simply, they have found a person they can relate to culturally, linguistically, and now emotionally.

They don't see me as American anymore. They see me as Arab, but more so. "There's a rumor going around the camp that you are Palestinian. Is that true?" My heritage mattered to me more than ever now, because now the Syrians are feeling what the Palestinians have felt for so many years: a world watching silently as they are slaughtered and forced out of the lands they so dearly loved for generations.

For the most part, the children were overly-anxious at the idea of attending "school". For months, they had done nothing but wander around aimlessly: either getting into some type of trouble or walking into areas that weren't safe for them, such as the streets around the camps. Once we started, we would have young boys and girls waiting for us outside of the center. "Auntie Rasha, you guys are late. We've been waiting for you!" they would say in Arabic. The center opens at 9:00 am . . . it was 8:57 am.

The majority of the children behaved quite well, considering that many of them had never been in a school setting. But we could see the vast differences between those who had parents that were teaching their children on their own, versus the parents who had let all this time pass without teaching their child the basics, even how to hold a pencil. In addition, we were aware that we would encounter some behavioral issues, especially when one considers the trauma or PTSD that some of these children have been afflicted with. Every so often, we would have a scuffle, especially between the boys, but overall I was extremely pleased with how well the children were behaving.

Life would not be life without a little bit of drama. Unfortunately, in these kinds of situations, so many NGOs, groups and individual volunteers are swarming around, sometimes aimlessly. Each person or entity is trying to figure out what the hell is going on, and what their particular niche should be. As a direct consequence of different perceptions of the problems to be faced, the organizational bureaucratic constraints of each NGO and the different changing resources at hand, some conflicts and differences in opinion or policy arise. Over the course of my different assignments working with refugees in different locations and different countries around the world, I have seen the good, the bad and the ugly.

As Dr Kathy Stolarz has said in her chapter, when we all work together, amazing things can happen. But at other times, petty rivalries between different NGO's can get in the way. Sometimes dysfunctional, if not catastrophic consequences can result. See Dr Bill Dienst's chapter about balancing our Souls between our Hearts and Minds. At the end of that chapter, he gives an example of a breakdown in cooperation between rival NGOs, which resulted in an unnecessary closure of a fully operational free standing clinic at Eko camp. This was not the first time, nor the last, that such episodes have occurred.

The biggest problem by far, one that can only truly be understood when witnessed first-hand, is the ego problem. It seems like the bigger the NGO, the bigger the ego. From what I have seen, smaller groups worked quite well together most of the time, although admittedly, not always. Smaller organizations do have the advantage of being able to move in quickly and address a problem. But they often lack the resources to build larger infrastructures.

The larger NGO's are often more bureaucratically unwieldy and take longer to respond. To me, it appears that the smaller NGO's were on the ground, addressing a need in a quarter of the time, while big NGO's were wasting time simply doing paperwork to get "approval" from their supervisors. At some of the camps, once they did finally respond, some of the better-known NGOs didn't want to play nice or fair with the smaller NGO's that had preceded them in the task at hand. This was very frustrating to those of us volunteering with the smaller NGOs. It seemed like a petty power grab, silly and immature. Many times it appeared that the refugees were the ones paying the price.

For example, I was able to open two learning centers at the military camps earlier on. But this was followed later on by these learning centers being stripped away from me by bigger NGOs who stepped in and pushed smaller groups out of projects that the larger NGOs themselves should have started months earlier. At times, it makes one wonder about ultimate motivations. Who is there to truly help these stranded refugees, and when does power and ego get in the way?

During the majority of the summer, Frakapor camp lacked many basic needs compared to other camps, because there were no actual humanitarian groups left inside anymore as a result of the head-butting and bickering. The groups, which had been pushed out, including SCM, would operate from outside the gates, handing out bread, dates, sugar, vegetables, etc.

Many of the refugees had my number just in case there was an emergency. But mainly they just wanted to say hello and send me selfies of them and their friends. On one particular night however, I received a call from a family in Frakapor whose father received dialysis three days a week. I knew Abdullah very well because I'd been called to his tent before. He sat in front of me vomiting clear liquid into a bucket over and over, barely able to keep his head up. He could barely say my name without the need to put his head back in the bucket. His hands and feet were swollen three times their size.

Previously, Abdullah and another dialysis patient were taken to the hospital for their treatment, but they were not provided a ride back. They were forced to take a bus to the nearest stop and had to walk over an hour back to the camp. A medical group asked me to speak to him over the phone. They wanted me to try to convince him to go to the hospital. He adamantly refused to go, and for good reason, based on the ordeal he had been through previously. I told the coordinator I would be willing to go to the camp and speak to him face-to-face so that I could convince him that he needs to go to the ER.

Her response baffled and angered me: "We don't need to go to the camp. It's childish to have to convince an adult they need to go to the hospital." She kept repeating the word childish as she sat on the comfortable couch drinking her coffee and enjoying the air conditioning. She insisted that during her actual job back in the UK that this never happens, they don't go running around after people to go see a doctor. At this moment, she seemed to me to show arrogance and ignorance. Perhaps she was feeling burned out from being confronted by too many overwhelming medical needs all at once and not having enough time to process them all. She seemed to have lost track of the situation that she herself had volunteered to help in.

These people are in a foreign country. They don't speak the language. They barely have any money. They've experienced being stranded at the hospitals, repeatedly. Many are already suffering from some form of pre-existing trauma due to their journey and many now suffer from depression. This is not your average situation. I went the next morning to check up on him. He was still very ill and laying inside the tent with two medical volunteers. It turned out he had sepsis and ended up in the hospital for one month. His wife never left his side. At times, I would go to the camp and bring his sixteen year old son to visit him, leaving his twelve year old sister behind.

"We want to get smuggled out. He cannot stay here any longer in these conditions because he will die. I cannot live without him." This is what his wife would constantly cry to me. For the entire month, I visited the hospital on average twice a week late at night. Sometimes the Greek doctors would call in at 1:00 am or 3:00 am asking me to translate over the phone or actually come in for an emergency with him. During that entire month, not one time did any of the doctors from the volunteer groups in the camp ever ask to come to the hospital with me. Perhaps they felt overwhelmed by the immediate present needs within the camps, and they had to rely on the Greek doctors at the hospital to handle the inpatient needs.

But technically he was still their patient, and I have zero medical training. I would Skype with my husband, who is a flight medic in our town of Columbia, Missouri, and ask him what questions I should be asking the doctors and show him the patient's swollen feet and areas of infection for his opinion.

I worked with the UNHCR coordinator of that camp attempting to get Abdullah and his family removed and placed into temporary housing while their paperwork was being filed. They had him listed as an urgent case, due to his severe medical condition. Yet almost five months later he is still in Greece. At one point he ended up in the hospital again for another month due to a pneumonia infection. The paperwork is taking an unusually long time to be processed, and there is practically nothing I can do about it.

The connections to those in the camps can be endless. It's as if at every turn, there is a surprise! And good or bad, you have to deal with it. Undoubtedly, the most frustrating of these issues is the painfully slow process of getting these families settled in other countries, which have promised to take in a certain amount of refugees, but so far have either taken in none or only a small percentage. The worst are the cases involving children. One in particular was mentioned in Dr Kelly Griffin's chapter:

Hammoudi and his family were on a bus fleeing from Damascus when their bus was caught in the raging crossfires between Syrian government forces and DA'ISH (ISIS). Nearly everyone was slaughtered by the raging bullets firing through both sides of the bus. Hammoudi was shot in the head.

He currently still has bullet fragments in his head, and to make matters worse, he lost part of his skull where he was shot. Since there is no skull bone in the area, his brain bulges out. If one simply moves his hair to the side, you can see the brain area not only swollen outward, but it also pulsates from the blood pumping through it. Still, Hammoudi behaves like any other normal child. He runs around, plays and rides a bicycle. Naturally, his mother is terrified, as am I, that he will fall and hit the affected area, or a ball will hit him in the head, or this or that. Anything can happen that can put this little boy in danger where he might suffer an adverse brain injury. And as with many of my other cases, I've been working on this with the UNHCR and other organizations to try to have his family not only relocated to a safer living condition, but also to get him into a country that has facilities to better take care of him, including a neurosurgeon that is willing to operate on him.

Then you have a single father of three, we'll refer to him as N, who I've known since Idomeni. I was thrilled to see that many of the people I've met in Idomeni were now relocated to the camps I work in. I noticed his demeanor had changed slightly. But that's normal considering the bleak reality of his situation. As the weeks went by, he seemed to be slipping into a depression as the separation from his wife for almost one year was becoming too much of a burden to bear.

His wife had reached Germany for asylum prior to the Macedonian border closing. A rarity in this camp, as one would usually find that the fathers had left first for asylum and the mothers are left alone with the children. By the time N left with his children, the borders had been closed. The strain of the distance and uncertainty about reunifying his family was becoming hard for him to endure. By the end of my trip in the summer, he was a stark contrast to the man, husband and father I had met back in April. N was falling into a deep depression. This became physically evident on his face. He had aged and the look of fatigue was all over his face. He stayed in his tent for days at a time. He wouldn't sleep. He wouldn't eat. He spoke of suicide daily in the hopes that if he killed himself the governments would be forced to reunite his wife and his children, since they are all minors. When I realized how serious N was becoming about killing himself, I immediately called the coordinator of a very well-known NGO to speak to a mental health specialist. His response? "Well, today is Thursday. The next time we are at the camp is Wednesday. I'll try to pass by tomorrow."

The weeks were passing by as were the issues that are part of such a situation—the food, the clothing, the education, the water, the bathrooms, and the medical aspects. The refugees have been living in a vicious cycle of repetitiveness. That feeling of the walls closing in on them never ends because there seems to be no end in sight. Every day is literally the same, like the movie "Groundhog Day," but even much worse. It is like some sort of sick mind-game. They wake up, get unhealthy food from the military, sit in front of the their tent, look at their phones, maybe walk around, talk to some people and stay up all night talking some more. This repeats itself for days and weeks and months. It's monotonous. People, especially the men, felt useless. One man from the Kalachori camp said to me, "The women, at least, they are busy with the children and cooking. But us men, what are we to do? We have no jobs. We are losing our minds here. We can't even support our families. We don't feel like men anymore."

I have had many first-hand experiences from my time traveling to various camps in different countries. I have been exposed to refugees from different cultures. Two major impressions stand out:

The first is the serious and alarming delay of large NGOs. When I first arrived in Lesvos during the fall of 2015, it was practically barren with no sign of life from the larger and more financially capable NGOs that we see so much on social media showcasing how they've been assisting the refugees. This can be said for their presence in the camps in both Greece and France. I was shocked, angry and confused. Why were they not here in a much stronger presence? Where is all the donated money going? Part of me was feeling alienated by what I will call "the NGO Industry". Have they put more effort into making a name for themselves through marketing and printing booklets and empty tubs with their names on them rather than investing in the proper care of these refugees? Or are they simply being spread too thin by all the humanitarian crises that are afflicting our world today?

The second insight is the simple fact that most countries, which have promised to take in thousands of refugees, have barely done so. We pride ourselves on learning from history so as to not repeat our mistakes. We pride ourselves on standing up for human rights, but what it really seems to be is that we only stand up for certain humans' rights. Our support, including financial, depends on who it's going towards. What color are they? What religion do they practice? What region of the world do they come from?

Our world is no Utopia; far from it. It seems hopeless at times. I've grown impatient in many ways, either with the situation as a whole, or the politics of it, or simply even with people's arrogance regarding these refugees. Now we have the rhetoric of Donald Trump and growing anti-refugee sentiments from right wing political parties in Europe.

Yet I find that humanity still exists, even in the simplest of forms. Whether it be a simple smile from a Swiss volunteer to a Kurdish refugee from Syria, or from an elderly Afghan woman who softly grabbed my face and pulled it gently down to hers, kissing my cheeks as she spoke to me in her mother tongue that I could not understand. But the smile on her face and tears in her eyes said what words could not convey on that day on the shore of Lesvos. Humanity still exists.

It still thrives among the refugees themselves and the dedicated volunteers that I've met from SCM, Swiss Cross Help (an amazing group we work with in the camps), or to the countless others here who are volunteering out of the kindness of their hearts. They have all taught me what it is to be resilient. They have taught me true lessons in compassion:

The refugee who lost practically his entire family in a barrel bombing in Syria . . . the refugee who fled Afghanistan with his family because of terrorist groups slaughtering people . . . or the refugees who rode on a raft with dead bodies on it. We can all learn something from them and that is simply their persistence and their will to live.

Four days ago, I returned to Greece. One day, I hope this huge refugee crisis in Greece and many other countries will be peacefully resolved. I would like to be able to someday visit this beautiful country of Greece for a reason other than working in refugee camps.

Resources

Epilogue

February 2017
Madi Williamson, Dr. Bill Dienst, Dr. Kathy Stolarz, Mohammed J. Deen, Rasha Abousalem.

At the beginning of July 2016, the UN's refugee agency (UNHCR) began the first steps of a lengthy process to legally register the residents of the military camps in Greece and place them in new host countries in the European Union, and elsewhere, where they hope to receive asylum.

Months ago, the unofficial camps like Eko and Idomeni were bulldozed to the ground. Now there are no obvious signs of refugees in the farmer's fields of Idomeni or the parking lot of an Eko gas station outside the town of Polykastro; places that were once teeming with tents for thousands of refugees. Memories will always be engrained in the hearts and minds of those of us who came to know these places: bustling communities of people who became our friends, not just white noise along the highway in the mountainous scenery that stretches between Thessaloniki and the Greece/Macedonia border.

Now the military camps around Thessaloniki are slowly being evacuated too. People are moving to apartments in the area, or to Athens. There, they meet with representatives from UNHCR and are eventually informed of their new asylum country at their third appointment following pre-registrations. This is then followed by an interview. The process takes months. Although many of the military camps that SCM and SAMS have worked in are emptying and closing down, NGOs and local law enforcement are anticipating that some of the other camps will remain open to take in new residents sent to the mainland from the Greek Islands in the spring of 2017.

Henry (not his real name) was one of our translators. He grew tired of lingering in the military camps after the forced displacement of Eko Camp. He finally paid smugglers to get him transported to another country on the northern shore of the Mediterranean in the fall of 2016. He then made it overland to Germany, where now he is happily reunited with his brother and his brother's family who have already been living in Germany for over a year.

Vincent (not his real name) was another one of our translators. His story is featured in an earlier chapter of this book. He has moved to Athens, given up on notions of reuniting with family in Germany, and is now applying for asylum in New Zealand.

Nour is the young woman who helped us translate in the woman's clinic in Eko. Greek police evacuated her and her brother from Eko camp in June 2016 along with other refugees. She found conditions in the first military camp where they were taken intolerable. They relocated to Lakathika camp in Thessaloniki, where they have since applied for asylum and await their next asylum interview (still pending in April 2017. At times there is not enough food, and Nour looks for a reason to go on, but she is strong and finds purpose in caring for her little brother and her friend's children.

Alyamman is the young boy from Eko camp with a progressive neuromuscular disorder who was at death's door in May 2016. As described in a previous chapter, he moved to a pediatric specialty hospital in Switzerland from Athens by commercial airliner while receiving medical support from a volunteer who escorted him all the way from Eko Camp. He has since stabilized and been discharged from the hospital. The family also relocated and they are living a better life in Switzerland now. Unfortunately, his baby sister apparently suffers from the same disorder, suggesting a possible genetic link.

Hammoudi is the young boy who suffered a gunshot wound to the head, while riding in a bus on his way to Damascus, and suffered from a persistent open skull wound. After months of tedious and persistent work by dedicated volunteers and an evaluation by a Greek neurologist, he and his family were finally granted humanitarian visas in November 2016 by the Swiss government. He transferred to a pediatric specialty hospital in Switzerland where he recently received neurosurgical closure of his skull wound. Expectations are that he should have a complete recovery.

N is the single father of three whose wife reached Germany while the rest of the family was stuck in the military camp in Greece. He was suffering with morbid depression. Unfortunately, this case has taken a turn for the worse. Insisting on going to Germany where his wife is, this father went through the German embassy instead of the usual UNHCR route. When he retrieved his passports and gave back his UN ID cards, he signed paperwork, which he did not fully understand, stating that he knowingly and willingly forfeited his asylum rights in Greece and had fifty days to leave Greece. Otherwise, he would be considered an illegal, and if caught, could face two months jail time.

Currently his NGO caseworkers are franticly compiling all the paperwork needed for the German embassy in Greece, while stalling the Greek authorities from taking legal action against him. They have also been consulting with lawyers as well as the well-known group Solidarity Now. Presently, his caseworkers have several days to figure out how to have the family's reunification paperwork approved by the German government. On a positive note, the father's depression has massively improved. His wife and mother of his children received permission from Germany to travel to Greece and finally saw her husband and children after over one year of separation.

For some, long journeys as refugees in Greece are ending as they finally arrive in their new host countries. Others still linger in Limbo, and for others, the refugee ordeal is just beginning.

Arrivals from Turkey still flow into the islands . . . not in the numbers we saw in 2015 and early 2016, but still enough to cause public health concerns. The small camps on the Greek Islands are again being pushed further and further beyond what they were designed to hold.

The most recent updates from the Greek Ministry of Health show that the camps on the islands of Leros, Chios, Samos, and Lesvos are again all over capacity by at least 1500 residents. Meanwhile, the big camps around Thessaloniki like Frakapor,

Karamanlis, and Vasilika are at 50-300 people, when just six months ago they each swelled to 800-1500 residents.

The flow of refugees leaving the endless wars in Syria and other countries in the Middle East has not halted; it has only been re-routed, as it has so many times before, since the first group of refugees fled to Jordan seeking safety in 2011. With no end to the civil-proxy wars in sight, it is still unclear when we will see the end of this massive humanitarian disaster. Dedicated volunteers and organizations will continue to assist the displaced seeking refuge in any way that we can.

Notes

1. From "Starry Starry Night," Don McLean's ballad about Vincent Van Gogh. Don McLean, 1972.
2. See "Fear is a Powerful Stimulant," by Dr. Bill Dienst. *Electronic Intifada*: https://electronicintifada.net/content/fear-powerful-stimulant-part-1/6644
3. Robert F. Kennedy Jr. "Why the Arabs don't want us in Syria," *Politico*: 16 September 2016.
4. Matt Schiavenza. "How ISIS Shook Off al Qa'ida and Became Even More Powerful in Iraq," *International Business Times*: 17 June 2014.
5. Kennedy Jr. Op Cit.

NGO Disclaimer

Acknowledgements

There are so many people who helped us along this long voyage and the realization of this book, they are too numerous to completely mention.

Nevertheless, we want to thank our proofreaders, Barbara Bodden and Greta Berlin. Just when we thought we had the "perfect" manuscript, our proofreaders pointed out about 500 imperfections to fix. We also want to thank our publisher Scott Davis at Cune Press. After we survived the initial proofread, Scott pointed out about ten dozen more imperfections. The result is this very high quality book.

Thank you to Jim Williamson for spending tedious hours perfecting our maps to lend some context for the content of the chapters.

We want to thank Rita Zawaideh, the CEO, and Brenda Pierce, the Mission Coordinator for Medical and Humanitarian Volunteers at Salaam Cultural Museum in Seattle who sent so many of us volunteers on the trajectory of this life-altering voyage from which we will never be the same. In addition, we thank Basel Sawalha from Madaba, Jordan, who is the Regional Director for SCM and who helped us get situated both in Lesvos and in Northern Greece.

Thank you to the members of the refugee communities who came forward to help us with translations in the unofficial camps, Eko and Idomeni, as well as in the military camps, Frakapor, Iliadis, Karamanlis and Vasilika.

On Lesvos, we acknowledge and express our gratitude to the other NGOs operating alongside us in Molyvos: Medics Bergen, Starfish, and many others as well as all of the organizations running the two camps Moria and Kara Tepe in Mytilene. We thank Mr. Savvas, our host and the employees at the Hotel Panselinos on the northern shore of Lesvos who allowed us to transform their hotel into the region 1 logistics center for rescue operations in the North.

In Northern Greece, we want to thank Dr Jolien Colpaert, the coordinator of Medecins Sans Frontiers and all her colleagues at MSF who had the insight to work collaboratively with many NGOs, large and small, like bricks and mortar, making the impossible a workable reality.

Thanks to Dr Siyana Shafi of Kitrinos Healthcare (Off Track Health) and her administrators, Anna McPhee and Mairi Calder who showed Dr Bill the ropes of running mobile health clinics in the mud of Idomeni's farm fields, kept him in line, and then put him in charge. Also head nurse Thorrin Morrow who did his most to keep Dr Bill level-headed while we all tried our very best to make order out of chaos and not lose our mindfulness.

In addition, Dr Georgios Perperidis, dentist and medical director at Polykastro Health Center who worked with us collaboratively to help us provide some lab and dental services for refugees amid overwhelming needs. Also, Petros Tsetris, our Greek volunteer who provided critical liaison work and Greek/English translation which pulled us through many difficult situations innumerable times.

We owe a hearty thanks to the support of Greek authorities, both police and military, for their role in keeping aid workers and the refugee population as safe as possible in the harsh circumstances we faced. Thank you to WE ACT Sweden and Kitrinos Healthcare for the ambulances that served as the primary care and women's clinics in Eko camp, to our colleagues at Medicine de Monde, Doctors without Borders, International Rescue Committee, The Red Cross, Swiss Cross Help, Save the Children, UNHCR, and to their partners for the medical, humanitarian, and logistical support. Your aid was hugely beneficial to the refugee population and to smaller organizations operating in both the unofficial camps in the north and in the military camps around Thessaloniki.

We would also like to recognize and praise the tireless work of Dr. Matthias Keller of Switzerland who has helped many refugees get the medical care that they need. He was the man behind the mission to evacuate the young boy from Eko to Switzerland where he received life-saving medical intervention. He was also one of the friendly faces to show us the ropes upon our arrival in Idomeni in March of 2016.

Thanks to SAM's in-country coordinator Katerina Nickolopoulos and Dr. Afsana Safa, who took over the reins from Dr. Bill in May 2016 and brilliantly managed the continuation of care in the unofficial camps and the transition into the military camps. Thank you also to Nikki Pallas, Leo Nauomis, Dr. Meghan Gunst, and Dr. Zareena Mohamed for their work in establishing the clinics and transport system of patients in the military camps. Many lives were improved because of your hard work and dedication to the refugee community. You saw them as not only our patients, but also as our friends, providing them with incredibly meaningful care inside and outside of the clinic.

Thanks to the owners and employees of the Park Hotel in Polykastro, who offered a meeting place for volunteers to plan and organize; warm food, and good company. Also to the owners and employees of the Hotel Maison and Hotel Perinthos who nurtured us, gave us places to come home to and sustenance at the end of physically and emotionally draining days in the North of Greece.

Finally, we want to thank all our co-workers, our brothers and sisters, both humanitarian and medical. Thanks to all of these volunteers who came to help others in need, whether you came with an organization, as an independent, or as a member of the refugee population stepping forward to help. Your impact was essential. And thanks to the families of these volunteers for their support keeping the home fires burning while their loved ones were away in Greece.

Authors

Bill Dienst, MD and **Madi Williamson** (See page 154)

Jamal Sawalha is from Jordan. He was the Logistics Manager and Team Leader for Salaam Cultural Museum Medical Missions in Greece from October 2015 to August 2016. Prior to that, he worked with SCM in Jordan for three years. His God-mother, Rita Zawaideh is the founder of SCM, which is based in Seattle, Washington, USA. Jamal studied Logistical Sciences at the German-Jordanian University, and spent over a year studying in Germany. He speaks Arabic, German and English. His ability to speak this combination of languages has proven extremely valuable. SCM activities are coordinated with many other international NGOs including those Switzerland, Austria and Germany, which are dedicated to providing medical and humanitarian aid to the refugees in Greece.

Amer Alhaj is from Deir ez-Zor, Syria. He is one of the thousands of refugees stranded in Northern Greece following the closing of the border from Greece to the Former Yugoslavian Republic of Macedonia. Amer learned English during his time at University where he studied engineering. He has since expanded his knowledge of the language by volunteering with medical personnel in the camp he lives in, and by writing poetry to go with his photos. He started a Facebook page to share his work called *Refugees on Route*.

Raafia Gheewala Pharm D is a pharmacist from Massachusetts with a passion for humanitarian aid. She volunteered in Lesvos, Greece providing medical and humanitarian relief work with the refugees. She was affiliated with the Seattle based NGO, SCM.

Kirsten Senturia PhD is a medical anthropologist who conducts community assessment and program planning with immigrant and refugee communities in Washington State. She volunteered in Lesvos, Greece in February and March, 2016 with SCM.

Lindsey Smith (FNP) is a Nurse Practitioner from Minneapolis, Minnesota with a passion for hospice and palliative care. After witnessing a disparity in culturally sensitive care for Muslim families in Minnesota, she decided to work towards building bridges for end-of-life care in this population. This led to travels in the Middle East where she was awakened to the Syrian refugee crisis. This article is based on her recent volunteer work with the Syrian American Medical Society (SAMS), a US based NGO, in refugee camps in northern Greece along the Macedonian border. She continues to advocate for victims of the Syrian Civil War.

Katherine Stolarz DO is a Family Medicine physician providing adult, pediatric, and obstetric/gynecologic care in Baltimore, Maryland, and is an Assistant Professor at Georgetown University. Her areas of focus include Women's Health and Global Health, with ongoing projects in Central America. She also provides asylum evaluations to asylum seekers in the United States, and trains Family Medicine residents and medical students in ethical global medical efforts. Dr Stolarz worked with refugees in Idomeni, Greece, through Salaam Cultural Museum.

Ahmed Younso is a twenty-nine-year-old teacher and poet from Daraa, Syria. He volunteered in Eko, Idomeni and other military camps as a translator and teacher for more than nine months with different organizations. Through his poetry, he tries to show new subjective perspectives of what it feels like to be a refugee.

Mohammad J Deen is currently a Nurse Anesthesia Resident training in northern California. Having had extensive medical background working in various intensive care units in Chicago as an RN, as well as working in EMS in the pre-hospital setting as a Medic/RN on the streets, Mohammad decided to take on his next journey to work with Syrian Refugees in Europe. Having had previous experiences with projects in West Africa, humanitarian work has always been a passion for him. Mohammad spent nearly three months in northern Greece, volunteering with the UK based NGO called Kitrinos. Most nights, Mohammad covered Eko camp as the sole provider for nearly 3000 people. It has been an experience that he talks about until this day. His mini-film "No place like HOPE" raises awareness to the daily struggles the refugees experience in Greece. His hope is that the film will bring about more awareness and advocate on behalf of refugees and their plight.

Kelly Griffin MD is a critical care physician from California, now living in New Jersey, and working in New York. She has so far taken two trips to northern Greece to work as a camp clinic physician with Syrian refugees through the Syrian American Medical Society (SAMS), which provides medical care to refugees in Syria, Lebanon, Jordan, and Greece. She plans to continue working with refugees and asylum-seekers indefinitely within the United States as well as future mission trips abroad. She has previously worked as a physician in Red Cross shelters in Louisiana after Hurricane Katrina.

Tim Spenser is from Bainbridge Island, Washington. He and his mother, Ellin, whose paternal grandparents emigrated from Lesvos in the early 20th century, were humanitarian volunteers with Salaam Cultural Museum during the first two weeks of December, 2015. Tim studied Political Economy and Social Movements at the Evergreen State College in Olympia, Washington, from which he graduated in 2010. He currently lives and works in Boulder, Colorado.

Rasha Abousalem is the daughter of Palestinian refugee parents, now living in the United States. Rasha was raised to embrace both her American and Palestinian sides. She received a degree from John Jay College in New York City, having majored in International Criminal Justice with concentrations on human rights and refugees. She is fluent in conversational Arabic and has used her skills and experiences in the refugee crises in Jordan, Greece, and France to bring humanitarian relief. Most recently, she has been introducing educational components in camps through Salaam Cultural Museum. In addition to volunteering for SCM, Rasha also served as the Director of Humanitarian Operations for Global First Responder (GFR), a NGO based in Columbia, Missouri. She has also traveled to remote Indian villages with GFR to offer medical and humanitarian assistance. She plans to continue her work in refugee camps and to join other volunteer trips to various locations in the coming years.

Abdulazez Dukhan is an eighteen-year-old from Homs, Syria. He and his family fled to Turkey as the war in their home city intensified, and in March of 2016, they made the crossing to Greece only to face closed borders. As a refugee living in Greece, Abdulazez took up photography and launched his own social media page, *Through Refugee Eyes,* focusing on raising awareness and sharing the truth about the reality for the refugees living in Greece.

The Syrian American Medical Society (SAMS) is a non-profit, non-political, professional and medical relief organization that represents Syrian American medical professionals in the United States. SAMS is working on the front lines of crisis relief in Syria and neighboring countries to alleviate suffering and save lives. Through its rich network within the United States and in Syria, SAMS organizes medical missions to the region, provides professional and educational trainings to Syrian physicians, and delivers medicine and medical supplies to hospitals and vulnerable families.

Kitrinos Healthcare is a team made up of volunteer doctors, nurses, paramedics, and other allied health professionals from all over the world. They work with translators and non-clinical staff with the aim of providing medical care to refugees affected by the migrant crisis. Their clinics in Northern Greece are run by international volunteers and serve the refugee population that call the camps home.

Salaam Cultural Museum (SCM) is a charitable non-profit organization originally formed in February 1996 to gather and publish information on the Middle East and North Africa and to promote understanding of the people, cultures, languages, and lands of this region. For the last several years they have been collecting and distributing humanitarian aid and coordinating medical missions to the region. Their current mission is on aiding the displaced Syrians who have fled the violence in Syria to neighboring countries.

Index

Bill Dienst, MD is a rural family and emergency room physician from Washington State. He has extensive experience in medical exchange programs in Veracruz, Mexico, as well as the West Bank and Gaza Strip in the Middle East. He has recently worked as the medical coordinator for Salaam Cultural Museum (SCM) in Lesbos and Idomeni, Greece. SCM is a Seattle based non-profit organization conducting humanitarian and medical relief work with refugee populations in Jordan, Lebanon and Greece. He previously co-edited and co-authored the book Freedom Sailors, which is about the maiden voyage of the Free Gaza Movement.

Madi Williamson is a humanitarian from Bainbridge Island, Washington. She has spent over two months working in the refugee camps in northern Greece with SCM. She was inspired to travel to Greece to help with the refugee crisis after successful medical missions to the Dominican Republic and founding her own charity to bring soccer equipment to orphans in Africa and South America. She is the founder of In-Sight, an organization aiming to provide educational and outreach tools to people wishing to learn more about the refugee crisis and other humanitarian disasters.

Made in the USA
Lexington, KY
06 April 2017